Other Kaplan Books of Interest to Parents of High School Students

Conquer the Cost of College

Kaplan/Newsweek *College Catalog*

High School 411

Parent's Guide to College Admissions

Yale Daily News *Guide to Summer Programs*

High Stakes High School: A Guide for the Perplexed Parent

by

Allison Zmuda, Mary Tomaino, and Jeanetta Miller

Simon & Schuster

NEW YORK · LONDON · SINGAPORE · SYDNEY · TORONTO

Kaplan Publishing
Published by Simon & Schuster
1230 Avenue of the Americas
New York, NY 10020

For bulk sales to schools, colleges, and universities, please contact Order Department, Simon & Schuster, 100 Front Street, Riverside, NJ 08075. Phone: 1-800-223-2336. Fax: 1-800-943-9831.

Project Editor: Megan Duffy
Contributing Editor: Seppy Basili
Editorial Coordinator: Dea Alessandro
Educational Research Associate: Rudy Robles
Cover Design: Cheung Tai
Interior Page Design and Production: Jan Gladish
Production Editor: Maude Spekes
Desktop Publishing Manager: Michael Shevlin
Executive Editor: Del Franz

Manufactured in the United States of America
Published simultaneously in Canada

September 2001
10 9 8 7 6 5 4 3 2 1

ISBN: 0-7432-1268-1

Table of Contents

Section I: Understanding Standardized State Tests

Section II: Opening the Lines of Communication

Section III: Appendixes: Information for Parents

About the Authors

Allison Zmuda, **Mary Tomaino**, and **Jeanetta Miller** represent three generations of high school teachers. Each has become an advocate for parental involvement. Allison Zmuda and Mary Tomaino are the authors of *The Competent Classroom*, a joint publication of the NEA and Teachers College Press, and Jeanetta Miller has written for *English Journal*.

Acknowledgments

This book is the result of our conversations with parents on the personal and national implications of standardized state tests on the secondary level. While parents that we spoke with were concerned about issues such as test preparation and accountability of school administration, they also wondered about whether teaching and learning benefited from the intensive focus on a single test. The philosophical questions parents raised were as influential in the shaping of *High Stakes High School* as the practical issues they asked to be addressed. We would like to thank those parents who spent their evenings with us shaping our manuscript: Deb Burkhart, Robert Burkhart, Nancy Cerreta, Richard Coopersmith, Monica DeFeo, Ann Deweese, Eileen Dunseith, Richard Dunseith, Bob Gaines, Carlen Gaines, Susan Hills, Chris Hoeffel, Natalie Hoeffel, Eitan Kilchevsky, Laurie Kilchevsky, Lynn Korotash, Kitty Latowicki, Kathy Nowak, Mike O'Connor, Janice Phelan, Bob Pious, Kathryn Simonds, Richard Simonds, Linda Sobo, Bill Wickson, George Wurtz, and Nancy Wurtz.

This book also is the result of our 50 years of collective teaching experience at Newtown High School in Sandy Hook, Connecticut. Through the generous support and professional development opportunities provided to us by our principal, William Manfredonia, and our assistant superintendent, Dr. Robert Kuklis, we have been able to extend our focus from our own curriculum and instruction to national educational issues.

We owe a debt of thanks to our editor, Maureen McMahon, for her genuine interest in responding both to public demand for a parents' guide on standards and state tests and to teacher efforts to create a meaningful learning experience for students. She is a true friend of all members of the school community and has been a strong advocate for strengthening the quality of American high schools.

Our husbands, Tom Zmuda, Rich Tomaino, and Charles Miller, graciously supported us through the long hours of discussions, writing, editing, and reshaping. They shared their perspectives as well as their hearts, and for that we are extremely grateful. Our children also have reminded us about the priorities we share as parents and as teachers. These reminders have helped us create a guide designed for parents that should also be read by every educator in the country.

Your Stake in High Stakes Testing

In 1983, the U.S. Department of Education's landmark report *A Nation at Risk* trumpeted the failure of American schools and called for drastic and immediate reform. The rise of the standards movement is a response to that call, culminating in an initiative established by national and state leaders called *Goals 2000*, which set eight goals for public schools. To assist schools in reaching these goals, the Department of Education drafted model standards in each area typically taught in school, and encouraged individual state departments of education to implement these standards in some form. Indeed, all states but Iowa have adopted state standards. (Iowa has elected to leave the responsibility to local districts.) Ideally, the state creates standards, aligns curricula with the standards, trains teachers, allows time for implementation in the classroom, and then administers a test that measures student achievement of the standards. Although use of standards for day-to-day work in the classroom has benefits for both students and teachers, problems arise when tests are administered before teachers and students are ready.

The batteries of state assessments that stem from the proliferation of standards at state and national levels are growing ever more important, not only to students, but also to school districts. The emerging wisdom seems to be that we should go ahead with standards and standardized state tests but be wary about attaching such high stakes to them. "High stakes tests," in a nutshell, are those that have real consequences—whether they be negative (summer school, retention, etc.) or positive (scholarships, additional funding for the school, etc.)—for the student, and, often, for the school as well.

The entire school team, central and school administrators and teachers, work together to ensure that the standardized test helps the school gather valuable information about student performance. They need to keep the community informed both before and after the test, determine how the district can make the best use of the testing process and results, train teachers efficiently and productively, and see that key skills to be tested are incorporated into teachers' daily lessons. The delicate balance must be maintained between teaching the curriculum and teaching the test but, when done well, standardized testing can refocus and strengthen public education.

So where does that leave you? Parents, whose role in education has traditionally been limited to bake sales and monitoring homework, have generally been left "out of the loop" in the development of standards. The purpose of this book is to help you understand the standards movement and its crucial role in your teen's education and to help you become an active partner in it. We hope that this book will serve parents of students who will increasingly be taking high stakes standardized assessments. It will provide you with information about how standards came about, how schools are using them now, and how you can become a valued participant in the continuing discussion.

You are entitled to accountability from your schools about what they have done and are doing to improve the quality of education. This book shows you how to ask for information about the standardized tests, both to become an active participant in the discussion of how to prepare students for the standardized testing and to help reinforce the work of the school at home.

The first section, "Understanding Standardized State Tests," provides a guide to the standards movement, tells you what you need to know about standardized state tests, and describes how schools prepare for them. These three chapters outline the origins of the standards movement, describe the role state and federal governments have played so far, and explain how you can stay current with changes in standards and testing for your state. Here it is important to note that the standards movement in education is changing and expanding rapidly. The examples that you read here are not set in stone, but indicate trends, patterns, and ideas.

In addition, the first three chapters explain the roles of the various groups in the school district: central and school administrators and teachers. Each has a distinct set of tasks to help the school prepare for the state test. When you try to familiarize yourself with the whole standardized test picture, it is helpful to know who has responsibility for what areas, so that you direct your concerns and questions in the appropriate direction.

Section two, "Opening the Lines of Communication," provides you with goals, protocols, and questions to use in initiating and continuing communication with teachers and administrators in your schools, with your own teenager, and with other parents. Since parents have been reluctant to intrude on the school's turf in terms of professional issues like testing, and since many parents and teachers are anxious about communicating with each other, we include specific strategies to increase your confidence and help to answer your questions and concerns. We also include strategies for communicating with your teenager; although your child is growing more independent every day, your interest still means a great deal and can reinforce the work of the school most positively. Finally, we suggest ways to get yourselves and other parents involved on an ongoing basis in the standards movement.

Because it is so important to speak the same language when sitting down at the table with school personnel, we have also included a glossary of key terminology and ideas about standards and testing in the "Information for Parents" section at the end of the book. It gives both definitions and suggestions for ways to clarify how the term applies in your teen's classes. Also included in the appendixes for your reference and further inquiry are state-by-state test surveys, Internet resources and other reading material, and more.

Dozens of public opinion polls and surveys resoundingly confirm that parents are an essential component of public education. Furthermore, parents who receive encouragement and training to become involved in standards work can make significant contributions to the school and community, and help to realize the full potential of the standards movement.

Fortified with the philosophy behind the standards movement, the practical knowledge of who does what, the strategies to get involved, and the key vocabulary, we hope that you will become a confident participant in the exciting changes going on in education. We also hope that *High Stakes High School* will help you join other parents to make your contributions even more significant.

UNDERSTANDING STANDARDIZED STATE TESTS

Chapter at a Glance

This chapter will outline the origins of the standards movement, describe the role that federal and state governments have played in the movement so far, and explain how you can stay current with changes in standards and assessment for your state.

Information

- Standards make it possible to measure student performance in the complex skills that are necessary in a rapidly changing world.
- Ideally, the state creates standards, aligns curricula with standards, trains teachers, allows time for implementation in the classroom, and then administers a test that measures student achievement of standards.
- Standards have been adopted in every state except Iowa, where the responsibility for creating standards has been consigned to local school districts.

Action

- Because state standards are revised every two to four years, parents need to keep up with current changes by communicating with their state department of education.

A Parent's Guide to the Standards Movement

1

You're half listening to the six o'clock news, half figuring out what to cook for dinner as you inch forward in the line of moms and dads picking up teens from field hockey practice. Your daughter spots the car, turns to wave good-bye to her teammates, and tosses her equipment bag and backpack in the trunk. She is glowing with exertion and carries the fragrance of fall air and clean sweat into the car with her. "Hi, sweetie," you say. "How was your day?"

"Practice was great," she replies, "I didn't let a single goal get past me, and Coach said I'll be starting at the next game."

"Wow!" you exclaim, "That's wonderful. How was school?"

"Oh, please!" she cries, "Don't remind me!" and bursts into tears.

"Honey! What's the matter?"

"My English teacher HATES me!"

There's only one correct reply to a pronouncement of this kind and you quickly make it. "I'm sorry you had such a rough time today. What happened?" Still sniffling, your daughter explains that she got a HORRIBLE grade on her essay, over which she had labored for HOURS, and that the teacher is NOT FAIR.

"I just don't understand what she wants," your daughter wails.

CHANGING THE COURSE OF HIGH SCHOOL

The idea behind academic standards is simple: Let students know what we expect of them in clear, specific language. However, some fundamental assumptions about the way education is delivered to students at the high school level had to change before standards could make sense to educators. Our vision of high school had to expand from the laudable goal of making information available to all American teenagers in an equitable and efficient way to the even more challenging goal of providing our teenagers with the problem solving and communication skills that are necessary in a rapidly changing world.

Most people would agree that high school should serve three purposes: to prepare teenagers for citizenship, to provide equal opportunity for economic advancement to all, and to instill in our young people an appreciation of culture in the United States and around the world. In a well-intentioned effort to make education equitable, educators worked for much of the 20th century to standardize curriculum and materials. The theory was that students in California, New York, and everywhere in between should have access to the same information and opportunities to learn.

Gradually we have realized that standardization of curriculum and materials is not only not enough, but it can also be counterproductive. When covering the curriculum becomes an end in itself, students spend too much of their time in school plodding chapter by chapter through textbooks and regurgitating their contents on multiple-choice tests. Standardized delivery of information can leach interest and relevance out of learning. Even worse, teaching essential skills such as reading, writing, and problem solving through a narrow focus on conventions and formulas deprives students of the aesthetic pleasures and power of language, and the thrill of genuine inquiry.

> *When covering the curriculum becomes an end in itself, students spend too much time methodically reading and regurgitating the contents of their textbooks.*

The release in 1983 of the Department of Education's *A Nation at Risk* made the problems with standardized delivery of information public. Educators realized that students needed, in Thoreau's words, "a broad margin to their lives." They needed opportunities, strategies, and encouragement to think, make connections, develop concepts, and communicate. We began to see reading, writing, and problem solving as integral to all subject areas, and approached them as processes that facilitated, deepened, and recorded the student's understanding and critical thinking. However, a new problem arose as we struggled with how to assess the student's achievement in these essential skills objectively. We began to see that we needed a coherent way to articulate our expectations, share them with students, and then use them as a guide in assessing student work.

Theorists and educators began to talk about why students should learn and what they should be able to do with their knowledge and skill. These discussions have resulted in momentous changes in educational philosophy. In science, for example, emphasis is shifting from rote acquisition of knowledge to learning through hands-on experimentation and application. According to the science framework developed by the Texas Education Agency (posted online at www.tea.state.tx.us/teks/), "students should know how science has built a vast body of changing and increasing knowledge described by physical, mathematical, and conceptual models, and also should know that science may not answer all questions." The TEA also noted that students need to study systems and patterns within systems so that they "understand a whole in terms of its components and how these components relate to each other and to the whole." And this understanding can come only from hands-on investigations. In fact, Texas' science framework specifies that 40 percent of instructional time be devoted to opportunities for students to conduct field and lab investigations that keep safety, the environment, and ethics in mind.

Standards are a way to express what we expect our high schoolers to know, and to assess their work objectively.

This desire for a change in teaching philosophy has been reinforced by the work of the U.S. Department of Education. Since the first educational summit meeting of state governors in 1989, the creation of challenging academic standards for all students has been a major goal of the Department of Education. It has created national task forces to draft standards in each area typically taught in schools, including art and physical education. These standards are available to states and localities that wish to adopt or adapt them. While the federal government cannot mandate the use of these standards, it has played an important role in the standards movement by supporting the development of model standards and providing a forum for diverse perspectives on education.

SETTING THE STANDARDS

Creating standards that are concise yet specific, rigorous yet accessible is a difficult, time-consuming process. Is all of this time and effort paying off in terms of increased student achievement? As noted in *Education Week*'s special report "Quality Counts 2001," the efforts of states to raise academic standards "are beginning to pay off where it counts: in the classroom. Test scores are rising in some states, many teachers report the expectations in their schools are climbing, and educators are slowly changing the curriculum to reflect state standards" (Edwards, 8). The potential for standards to result in lasting improvement in our schools is strong.

Academic standards are a work in progress, subject to revision as we learn more about what works and what doesn't. Informed, involved parents, like you, need to be part of this ongoing dialogue. In an article for *Clearing House*, Mary V. Bicouvaris, a member of the panel to determine national history standards, recalls the intense discussion over American history. At issue was whether the study of history should focus on common values and heritage or on the struggle of diverse groups for social justice and equality. The discussion went back and forth for almost a

> *The standards movement has provided us with a great opportunity for open dialogue.*

year, "with every talk show host and every barbershop gathering entering the debate." In June 1993, a compromise was reached that included both perspectives. One of the most significant benefits of the standards movement is the opportunity for open dialogue that it provides.

A similar debate has raged for some time over what should be included in language arts standards. On one side are those—such as E.D. Hirsch, professor, author, and founder of the Core Knowledge Foundation—who believe that literacy is achieved through knowledge of a specific list of works of literature, what is referred to by English teachers as "the canon." On the other side are those who believe that it is more important for students to read widely and with enjoyment than it is for them to read a prescribed list of books. People on this side of the debate want the latitude to compose a high school student's reading list from a combination of classic and contemporary works.

It is especially important to be aware of this debate as you look at Websites (such as those included in our Web Resource Directory in the back of the book) that evaluate each state's standards. Criteria for evaluation may differ from one organization to another. In addition, the criteria for evaluating standards are changing as we gain a better understanding of the important relationships between standards and standardized tests.

THE NEED FOR ALIGNMENT BETWEEN STANDARDS AND STANDARDIZED TESTS

Although all fifty states have adopted some form of standardized test to measure student achievement, vigorous debate continues about the value of standardized tests. Proponents argue that standardized tests *increase* learning because students and teachers are held accountable for the quality of their day-to-day work. Opponents argue that standardized tests *interfere* with learning because teachers teach to the test at the expense of other knowledge and skills. (In chapter 3 we discuss in more detail how schools prepare students for standardized assessments.)

Standards provide a middle ground on which proponents and opponents of standardizing testing can meet. When the standardized test is carefully aligned with standards for learning, there is no disconnect between the test and the work of students and teachers in the classroom. Forty-one states, such as Georgia and Louisiana, have adopted standardized tests aligned with standards in at least one high school subject area, typically English or math. However, the work is far from complete: Only half of the states have tests aligned with standards for history and science. Because alignment of standardized tests with standards is a work in progress, we want to emphasize that it is reasonable for you, as a parent, to ask how your state and local district are doing.

For each content area, states have developed standards for each key component. Using the extensive and impressive standards database on Achieve's Website (www.achieve.org), you can make a side-by-side comparison of standards in two different states. In mathematics, for example, both California and Florida have a section on probability. Although there are some variations in wording and in detail, both state departments have made a clear effort to indicate to educators what students are expected to know about probability and how they are expected to demonstrate that knowledge.

California State Standards, Grades 9–12 *Mathematics: Probability*	Florida State Standards, Grades 9–12 *Mathematics: Probability*
Probability and Statistics	**Data Analysis and Probability**
• Students know the definition of the notion of independent events, and can use the addition, multiplication, and complementation rules to solve for probabilities of particular events in finite sample spaces.	The student identifies patterns and makes predictions from an orderly display of data using concepts of probability and statistics.
• Students know the definition of conditional probability, and use it to solve for probabilities in finite sample spaces.	Students will: • Determine probabilities using counting procedures, tables, tree diagrams, and formulas for permutations and combinations.
• Students demonstrate understanding of the notion of discrete random variables by using them to solve for the probabilities of outcomes, such as the probability of the occurrence of five heads in fourteen coin tosses.	• Determine the probability for simple and compound events as well as independent and dependent events.
• Students are familiar with the standard distributions (normal, binomial, and exponential), and can use them to solve for events in problems where the distribution belongs to these families.	

The following comparison between New York and Kentucky state standards for science reinforces the basic similarities between states.

New York State Standards, Grades 9–12 *Science: Basic Features of the Earth*	Kentucky State Standards, Grades 9–12 *Science: Basic Features of the Earth*
Students will: • Use the concepts of density and heat energy to explain observations of weather patterns, seasonal changes, and the movements of the earth's plates. • Explain how incoming solar radiations, ocean currents, and land masses affect weather and climate.	Students will: • Examine how external sources of energy produce winds and ocean currents. • Examine how external sources of energy determine global climate.

While the similarities from state to state may be reassuring, it is important to note that coverage of the same topics is only part of the standards work. Other essential components of this effort include clarity of expectations for what students should know and be able to do, models of student work, scoring guides, sample test items, and special programs to help students who struggle to meet the standards.

The American Federation of Teachers (AFT) issues an annual study of state standards nationwide to determine what areas still need to be addressed to improve access, understanding, and achievement. Listed here are some of the major findings from their most recent report "Making Standards Matter 1999." (As these and other educational issues seem to be in a constant state of flux, you'll want to check the AFT Website, www.aft.org, for their next report, due to be released in July 2001.)

- Although standards have improved in many states, most states continue to have more difficulty setting clear and specific standards in English and social studies than in math and science.
- Through test items, scoring rubrics, and/or student work samples, many states (26) describe the level of mastery students must demonstrate to meet the state standards.

 9

- Fourteen states have policies for ending social promotion—the practice of passing students from grade to grade regardless of whether they have mastered standards. And 13 of those states link their promotion policy to the standards.

- More states with "minimum competency" exit exams are "upgrading" these tests to reflect 10th-grade standards or higher.

- Twenty-three states have or are developing incentives (advanced diplomas, free college tuition) to motivate students to achieve a higher standard than that required of all students.

- Since AFT's 1998 report, 29 states—an increase of nine—require and fund academic intervention programs for students who are struggling to meet the standards.

Education organizations nationwide agree that the standards movement has inspired tremendous efforts on national, state, and local levels to define what students should know and be able to do. But the establishment and enforcement of high standards is not enough. Educators also must ensure that all students are encouraged to meet high standards through the use of scoring guides, resources, clarity of language and communication, alignment of tests with standards, and availability of special programs. (For more information about how your teen's school fills these needs, see chapters 4 and 5 on communicating with teachers and administrators.)

The following six recommendations are also offered in the AFT's report.

AFT Recommendations for 1999

1. States need to improve their attention to the reading basics at the elementary level, especially in the primary grades (K–3), to include specific guidance on the basic knowledge and skills students should learn to develop into proficient readers.

2. Social studies standards need to be focused and explicit about the U.S. and world history that students should learn at each of the three educational levels.

3. Standards development is a continual process. Standards need to be revisited and revised as states delve deeper into standards-based curriculum development, aligned assessments, and standards-based professional development.

4. More work needs to be done on aligning assessments to the standards and in describing what adequate performance on the standards looks like.

5. All teachers and other stakeholders must have easy access to the standards and the full complement of clarifying documents and supplemental materials that states develop to illustrate the standards.

6. As more states implement "high stakes" policies based on the standards, programs must be in place to identify struggling students early in their school careers and to provide them with targeted academic assistance.

To read the full text of this study as well as to find a report on your own state's standards, go to www.aft.org/edissues/standards99/.

TAKING PART IN THE EVOLUTION OF STATE STANDARDS

As states continue to monitor and readjust their standards and tests, parents need to keep up with current changes. Your state standards will probably be revisited and revised every two to four years. New policies also will be instituted to reflect changes in philosophy, standards, and implementation. Because there is no guarantee that the test given last year will be the same this year, it is important to communicate with your state department of education.

Your state standards will probably be revised every two to four years.

Every state department of ed has a Website which offers a wealth of information and resources, often specifically targeted for parents. Most sites include the state content standards, testing schedules, testing policies, answers to frequently asked questions, and district-specific information.

The following chart includes the contact information for all 50 states as well as the District of Columbia. Because your state department of education will undoubtedly offer a daunting amount of information, it is important to generate a list of questions you have. Many of these questions can be answered simply by searching the Website, but if you need more personal attention, you can always call or fax them using the numbers provided in the chart below. Also, you'll find that almost all of these Websites offer you the opportunity to e-mail a question directly to the state department.

State Department	Address	Phone/Fax/URL
Alabama Department of Education	Gordon Persons Office Building 50 North Ripley Street P.O. Box 302102 Montgomery, AL 36130-2101	PHONE: (334) 242-9700 FAX: (334) 242-9708 URL: www.alsde.edu
Alaska Department of Education and Early Development	Suite 200 801 West 10th Street Juneau, AK 99801-1894	PHONE: (907) 465-2800 FAX: (907) 465-4156 URL: www.eed.state.ak.us
Arizona Department of Education	1535 West Jefferson Phoenix, AZ 85007	PHONE: (602) 542-5460 FAX: (602) 542-5440 URL: www.ade.state.az.us
Arkansas Department of Education	Room 304 A Four State Capitol Mall Little Rock, AR 72201-1071	PHONE: (501) 682-4204 FAX: (501) 682-1079 URL: arkedu.state.ar.us
California Department of Education	Second Floor 721 Capitol Mall Sacramento, CA 94244-2720	PHONE: (916) 657-2577 FAX: (916) 657-2682 URL: www.cde.ca.gov
Colorado Department of Education	201 East Colfax Avenue Denver, CO 80203-1704	PHONE: (303) 866-6600 FAX: (303) 830-0793 URL: www.cde.state.co.us
Connecticut Department of Education	Room 305 State Office Building 165 Capitol Avenue Hartford, CT 06106-1080	PHONE: (860) 566-5061 FAX: (860) 566-8964 URL: www.state.ct.us/sde/
Delaware Department of Education	John G. Townsend Building P.O. Box 1402 Federal and Loockerman Streets Dover, DE 19903-1402	PHONE: (302) 739-4601 FAX: (302) 739-4654 URL: www.doe.state.de.us
District of Columbia Public Schools	The Presidential Building 825 North Capitol Street, NE Washington, DC 20002	PHONE: (202) 724-4222 FAX: (202) 442-5026 URL: www.k12.dc.us
Florida Department of Education	325 West Gaines Street Tallahassee, FL 32399-0400	PHONE: (850) 487-1785 FAX: (850) 413-0378 URL: www.firn.edu/doe/

State Department	Address	Phone/Fax/URL
Georgia Department of Education	2054 Twin Towers East 205 Butler Street Atlanta, GA 30334-5001	PHONE: (404) 656-2800 (800) 311-3627 (in-state only) FAX: (404) 651-6867 URL: www.doe.k12.ga.us
Hawaii Department of Education	1390 Miller Street Honolulu, HI 96813	PHONE: (808) 586-3310 FAX: (808) 586-3320 URL: doe.k12.hi.us
Idaho Department of Education	Len B. Jordan Office Building 650 West State Street P.O. Box 83720 Boise, ID 83720-0027	PHONE: (208) 332-6800 (800) 432-4601 (in-state only) TTY: (800) 377-3529 FAX: (208) 334-2228 URL: www.sde.state.id.us/Dept/
Illinois State Board of Education	100 North First Street Springfield, IL 62777	PHONE: (217) 782-4321 TTY: (217) 782-1900 FAX: (217) 524-4928 URL: www.isbe.net
Indiana Department of Education	State House, Room 229 Indianapolis, IN 46204-2798	PHONE: (317) 232-6665 FAX: (317) 232-8004 URL: www.doe.state.in.us
Iowa Department of Education	Grimes State Office Building East 14th and Grand Streets Des Moines, IA 50319-0146	PHONE: (515) 281-3436 FAX: (515) 281-4122 URL: www.state.ia.us/educate/
Kansas Department of Education	120 Southeast 10th Avenue Topeka, KS 66612-1182	PHONE: (785) 296-3201 FAX: (785) 296-7933 URL: www.ksbe.state.ks.us
Kentucky Department of Education	1930 Capital Plaza Tower 500 Mero Street Frankfort, KY 40601	PHONE: (502) 564-3421 (800) 533-5372 (in-state only) FAX: (502) 564-6470 URL: www.kde.state.ky.us
Louisiana Department of Education	626 North Fourth Street P.O. Box 94064 Baton Rouge, LA 70704-9064	PHONE: (225) 342-4411 FAX: (225) 342-0193 URL: www.doe.state.la.us
Maine Department of Education	23 State House Station Augusta, ME 04333-0023	PHONE: (207) 624-6600 TTY: (207) 624-6800 FAX: (207) 624-6601 URL: janus.state.me.us/ education/

State Department	Address	Phone/Fax/URL
Maryland State Department of Education	200 West Baltimore Street Baltimore, MD 21201	PHONE: (410) 767-0462 FAX: (410) 333-6033 URL: www.msde.state.md.us
Massachusetts Department of Education	Educational Improvement Group 350 Main Street Malden, MA 02148	PHONE: (781) 388-3300 FAX: (781) 388-3396 URL: www.doe.mass.edu
Michigan Department of Education	Hannah Building Fourth Floor 608 West Allegan Street Lansing, MI 48933	PHONE: (517) 373-3324 FAX: (517) 335-4565 URL: www.mde.state.mi.us
Minnesota Department of Children, Families, and Learning	1500 Highway 36 West Roseville, MN 55113-4266	PHONE: (651) 582-8200 URL: cfl.state.mn.us
Mississippi State Department of Education	Suite 365 359 North West Street Jackson, MS 39201	PHONE: (601) 359-3513 FAX: (601) 359-3242 URL: www.mde.k12.ms.us/
Missouri Department of Elementary and Secondary Education	P.O. Box 480 Jefferson City, MO 65102-0480	PHONE: (573) 751-4212 TTY: (800) 735-2966 FAX: (573) 751-8613 URL: www.dese.state.mo.us
Montana Office of Public Instruction	P.O. Box 202501 Helena, MT 59620-2501	PHONE: (406) 444-2082 (888) 231-9393 (in-state only) FAX: (406) 444-3924 URL: www.metnet.state.mt.us
Nebraska Department of Education	301 Centennial Mall South P.O. Box 94987 Lincoln, NE 68509-4987	PHONE: (402) 471-2295 TTY: (402) 471-7295 FAX: (402) 471-0017 URL: www.nde.state.ne.us
Nevada State Department of Education	700 East Fifth Street Carson City, NV 89701	PHONE: (775) 687-9141 FAX: (775) 687-9101 URL: www.nsn.k12.nv.us/nvdoe/
New Hampshire Department of Education	101 Pleasant Street State Office Park South Concord, NH 03301	PHONE: (603) 271-3144 (800) 339-9900 (in-state only) TTY: (800) 735-2964 FAX: (603) 271-1953 URL: www.state.nh.us/doe/

State Department	Address	Phone/Fax/URL
New Jersey Department of Education	P.O. Box 500 100 River View Plaza Trenton, NJ 08625-0500	PHONE: (609) 292-4469 FAX: (609) 777-4099 URL: www.state.nj.us/education/
New Mexico State Department of Education	Education Building 300 Don Gaspar Santa Fe, NM 87501-2786	PHONE: (505) 827-6516 TTY: (505) 827-6541 FAX: (505) 827-6696 URL: sde.state.nm.us
New York Education Department	111 Education Building Washington Avenue Albany, NY 12234	PHONE: (518) 474-5844 FAX: (518) 473-4909 URL: www.nysed.gov
North Carolina Department of Public Instruction	Education Building 301 North Wilmington Street Raleigh, NC 27601-2825	PHONE: (919) 715-1299 FAX: (919) 715-1278 URL: www.ncpublicschools.org
North Dakota Department of Public Instruction	Department 201 600 East Boulevard Avenue Bismarck, ND 58505-0440	PHONE: (701) 328-2260 FAX: (701) 328-2461 URL: www.dpi.state.nd.us
Ohio Department of Education	Room 1005 25 South Front Street, 7th Floor Columbus, OH 43215-4183	PHONE: (877) 644-6338 FAX: (614) 644-5960 URL: www.ode.state.oh.us
Oklahoma State Department of Education	2500 North Lincoln Boulevard Oklahoma City, OK 73105-4599	PHONE: (405) 521-3301 FAX: (405) 521-6205 URL: sde.state.ok.us
Oregon Department of Education	255 Capitol Street, NE Salem, OR 97310-0203	PHONE: (503) 378-3569 TTY: (503) 378-2892 FAX: (503) 373-7968 URL: www.ode.state.or.us
Pennsylvania Department of Education	10th Floor 333 Market Street Harrisburg, PA 17126-0333	PHONE: (717) 787-5820 FAX: (717) 787-7222 URL: www.pde.psu.edu
Rhode Island Department of Elementary and Secondary Education	255 Westminster Street Providence, RI 02903-3400	PHONE: (401) 222-4600 FAX: (401) 222-6033 URL: www.ridoe.net

State Department	Address	Phone/Fax/URL
South Carolina Department of Education	1006 Rutledge Building 1429 Senate Street Columbia, SC 29201	PHONE: (803) 734-8492 FAX: (803) 734-3389 URL: www.state.sc.us/sde/
South Dakota Department of Education and Cultural Affairs	700 Governors Drive Pierre, SD 57501-2291	PHONE: (605) 773-3134 TTY: (605) 773-6302 FAX: (605) 773-6139 URL: www.state.sd.us/ deca/Education
Tennessee State Department of Education	Andrew Johnson Tower, 6th Floor 710 James Robertson Parkway Nashville, TN 37243-0375	PHONE: (615) 741-2731 FAX: (615) 532-4791 URL: www.state.tn.us/ education/
Texas Education Agency	William B. Travis Building 1701 North Congress Avenue Austin, TX 78701-1494	PHONE: (512) 463-9734 FAX: (512) 463-9008 URL: www.tea.state.tx.us
Utah State Office of Education	250 East 500 South Salt Lake City, UT 84111	PHONE: (801) 538-7500 FAX: (801) 538-7521 URL: www.usoe.k12.ut.us
Vermont Department of Education	120 State Street Montpelier, VT 05620-2501	PHONE: (802) 828-3147 FAX: (802) 828-3140 URL: www.state.vt.us/educ/
Virginia Department of Education	P.O. Box 2120 101 North 14th Street Richmond, VA 23219-2120	PHONE: (804) 225-2020 (800) 292-3820 (in-state only) FAX: (804) 371-2455 URL: www.pen.k12.va.us/ go/VDOE/
Office of Superintendent of Public Instruction (Washington)	Old Capitol Building 600 South Washington P.O. Box 47200 Olympia, WA 98504-7200	PHONE: (360) 586-6904 TTY: (360) 664-3631 FAX: (360) 753-6712 URL: www.k12.wa.us
West Virginia Department of Education	Building 6 1900 Kanawha Boulevard East Charleston, WV 25305-0330	PHONE: (304) 558-0304 FAX: (304) 558-2584 URL: wvde.state.wv.us

State Department	Address	Phone/Fax/URL
Wisconsin Department of Public Instruction	125 South Webster Street P.O. Box 7841 Madison, WI 53707-7841	PHONE: (608) 266-3108 (800) 441-4563 TTY: (608) 267-2427 FAX: (608) 267-1052 URL: www.dpi.state.wi.us
Wyoming Department of Education	Hathaway Building, Second Floor 2300 Capitol Avenue Cheyenne, WY 82002	PHONE: (307) 777-7675 FAX: (307) 777-6234 URL: www.k12.wy.us/ wdehome.html

Although many parents of teenagers never consider communicating with their respective state department of education, this point of contact is crucial in this new era of standardized tests. Not only will the department of education give you the latest updates on standards and testing, it will also be able to provide information about resources, public forums, and focus groups in your state and local areas. Before beginning your conversation on the state level, we recommend that you read chapter 2 to explore in more detail the fundamentals of standardized tests that all parents should know.

Chapter at a Glance

Chapter 2 will explain the purpose and benefits of standardized testing, discuss the use of standardized tests as a criterion for graduation, and explore the backlash that can occur when standardized tests are not aligned with standards and curriculum.

Information

- The standardized test helps the school gather information about student performance.
- Standardized testing can refocus and strengthen public education.
- Standardized tests are only one part of the standards reform package. All parts of the package need to be in place in order for standardized tests to be fair and effective.
- High stakes tests put some students at a disadvantage.

Action

- Advocate for change if you believe the standardized test used by your state has a negative impact on curriculum and learning.

What Parents Need to Know about Standardized Tests

As you sort through the mail, you come across an envelope addressed "To the parents of" your teenager, a sophomore. You expect to find a newsletter or a request for contributions to a bake sale. Instead, the envelope contains an official-looking document and a letter from the superintendent of schools. The letter explains that you have just received your teen's scores on the state's recently adopted standardized test. There are several sections to the test, the letter goes on. These sections include multiple-choice questions on editing and math and an extended response to litera-ture. "What's an extended response?" you wonder. Reading on, you realize that extended response is another way of saying "timed essay." "That'll be the day," you comment wryly, well aware that your wonderfully artistic and musical son has always frozen when asked to write essays under time pressure. Then you learn that your son's class is the first one for which successful completion of all sections of the state test will be required for graduation. Your heart starts to pound as you turn to the score report and try to figure out whether or not his score on the extended-response section meets the state goal. It does not. Your blood pressure soars from equal parts of anger and anxiety. "Why are they doing this to us!" you exclaim.

BENEFITS OF STANDARDIZED TESTING

Prior to the standards movement (see chapter 1), the quality of education varied dra-matically from one state to another and from one district to another. In the absence of consistently high standards and a system for holding schools accountable, students in some schools were expected to achieve at high levels while students in other schools passed through without learning much. Such fundamental inequity in education severely limits the opportunities for college and careers that are open to students who have the misfortune to attend schools that don't ask enough of them.

In the September 2001 issue of *American Teacher*, Sandra Feldman, president of the American Federation of Teachers, writes that "real standards reform—the kind that makes sure all kids get a rich curriculum, extra help if they need it to master the work, and tests that reflect the curriculum—is the most direct path to remedying long-standing inequities" (5). Feldman warns that in states where the only step that has been taken to reform education is implementation of a standardized test, there are "signs of backlash." The standardized test should be the last piece of the reform package to be implemented —after standards have been agreed on, the curriculum has been aligned with

When reforming education, the standardized test should be the last piece implemented.

them, and teachers have received professional development so they have the knowledge and strategies needed to make the standards-based curriculum a reality in the classroom. When these pieces are in place, standardized tests serve the purpose for which they were intended, which is in Feldman's words, "to measure progress and show us who needs help."

Test Format and Function

Standardized tests are composed of questions in one to three formats: multiple-choice, a short written constructed response, and a long written constructed response. As you can see from the following chart, adapted from the Maryland State Department of Education standards, each format has a specific function for the student and educator.

Format	Measurement of Achievement	Sample Assessment Item
Multiple-choice	Provides information about the student's knowledge in the areas tested	**ALGEBRA SECTION** A video store charges a one-time membership fee of $10.00 plus $2.50 per video rental. Which of these equations represents the amount (A) a customer spends, in dollars, for v videos? A. $A = 2.5v - 10$ B. $A = 2.5v + 10$ C. $A = 10v + 2.50$ D. $A = 10v - 2.50$
Constructed response— short written	Provides information about the student's knowledge in the areas tested and about reasoning and communication skills	**BIOLOGY SECTION** The concentration of salt in water affects the hatching of brine shrimp eggs. A scientist wants to determine the best conditions in which to hatch the shrimp eggs. In a laboratory, brine shrimp will grow at room temperature in small glass containers of salt water. Describe the steps of a *controlled* experiment that would determine the *best* saltwater concentration in which to hatch brine shrimp eggs. In your response, be sure to indicate: • The materials that will be used • The type of data that will be collected • How the data will be used to answer questions about the salt requirements of brine shrimp
Constructed response— long written	Provides information about the student's knowledge in the areas tested and a sample of the student's ability to reason and communicate	**GOVERNMENT SECTION** Explain how the media influence voters' opinions of political candidates. Include details and examples to support your explanation.

(Reprinted with permission from the Maryland State Department of Education. For further information, check out the Maryland State Department of Education Website at www.msde.state.md.us. Not only does the site provide access to sample assessments in each content area, but also includes the goals, expectations, indicators, and rubrics that the item is intended to measure.)

Some states still use "off the shelf" tests, such as the Stanford Achievement Tests, which consist exclusively of multiple-choice questions. However, most states have adopted more complex tests that are aligned with state standards for learning. In the State by State Survey at the back of this book you can look up your state to find out what type of standardized test is administered—as of press time. It is important to keep abreast of the current state of educational affairs in your state, and perhaps the easiest way to do so is to visit their Website often to check on field-testing and revised assessment design. Many states conduct extensive editing and reviewing efforts to ensure that the assessment accurately measures state content standards, remains up to date with curricula revisions, and provides all students with an equal opportunity to be successful.

The more constructed-response questions the test contains, the more detailed the information is that can be gained about the student's knowledge and ability to reason and communicate. However, scoring constructed-response questions is time-consuming and expensive. Forty-three states, including Illinois and Massachusetts, use standardized tests that feature a constructed-response section for English, whereas only five states use high stakes high school tests that include extended responses in other subject areas. While a few states, like Iowa and Kansas, still use tests that are 100 percent multiple-choice, most are striking a compromise between the need for more detailed information about student achievement and the cost of acquiring it.

Teaching the Test

The format, function, and consequences of these assessments may place educators and students in the hazardous territory of teaching to, and learning for, the test . . . and only the test. "Teaching to the test" can be a good thing if the test measures student performance on high-level tasks. However, all the parties involved must realize that a single test measures only some of the things that go on in a class-room over the long term, and not the full range of instruction. When we lose sight of that fact, we risk implementing a narrow and rigid curriculum and spending a year's instruction to influence the scores on a single test.

> *While "teaching to the test" can be worthy in some instances, it is important to remember that a single test measures only a portion of what goes on in a classroom.*

But the rewards of high performance on these standardized tests can often be great. Some states award diplomas with distinction or attach certificates of mastery to high school transcripts. As growing state-accountability rules pressure schools to prove that students are learning at ever higher levels, positive consequences can range from glowing press coverage to monetary rewards.

Publishing test scores can be a powerful incentive to refocus and strengthen education, and help to increase academic rigor in schools. Another positive aspect of publicized scores is diagnostic. In Chicago, school board president Gery Chico sees testing as "an intervention policy; test scores signal kids that need help, and what kind of help they need" (Rhodes, 43). One way Texas uses test scores is to evaluate programs, resources, and staffing patterns to direct attention and help where they are most needed (6).

It has been said that teachers generally teach what they like. Sometimes this has inspirational results, as when enthusiastic teachers galvanize students to love mathematics or Shakespeare. You probably remember, however, the World History teacher you had at one time who fell in love with the French Revolution and taught it for six months, giving life to the phrase "It's a small world." But standardized testing provides a level of accountability that was missing before. Teachers can no longer work in isolation. They have a responsibility to collaborate with colleagues, come to consensus about what students need to learn, and then follow through by teaching it in their classrooms.

A major benefit of standardized tests is the ongoing teacher training that state assessments generate. Giving teachers the opportunities to work with standards and encouraging them to integrate performance standards in their own daily planning works to raise the level of instruction overall, not just for a one-shot test. Encouraging teachers to work with colleagues to plan and write curriculum, moreover, allows teachers to enrich their own instruction and helps to ensure that students get more balanced and comparable instruction across subjects and grade levels. Collaboration increases a sense of trust and openness among teachers, and among teachers and administrators. All parties in the district share the obligation and desire to increase student performance (see chapter 3 for more on this). Because they are working together, even a disappointing result on the state assessment is not an opportunity to blame, but an incentive to pool their knowledge and expertise to solve the problems for the next year.

State assessments provide a new level of accountability and an impetus for raising the level of instruction in the classroom.

Standardized tests have been developed to fill a vacuum. Individual districts have not historically done well enough at proving that "the high school diploma really means something" (Olson, 30) and that schools are really doing their job. Most schools have not succeeded at the local level at systematically collecting data about student performance. When the public questions how the schools are doing—suspecting that the answer will be "not very well"—state tests can provide data to answer the question.

HIGH STAKES TESTS

At press time, 27 states, such as North Carolina, Texas, and New York, require students to pass the standardized test before promotion to the next grade, or graduation. These high stakes tests put pressure on all members of the school community—students, parents, teachers, administrators. Many politicians have swooped in on the practice of social promotion as one of the hallmarks of "our failing schools." However, the research makes it clear that retaining students doesn't work. Studies show that students who are required to repeat a grade are much more likely to give up and simply drop out of school. A parent in Connecticut voiced her concern about the pressure of high stakes testing on students like her daughter who are not good test takers. "I must confess that I am worried for some students if passing an exam becomes a criterion for graduation. This may inadvertently place an incredible amount of stress and become perhaps an unachievable goal for teenagers like my daughter who have been diagnosed with 'performance anxiety' and fail more tests than they pass." Placing too much emphasis on a single test sends a mixed message to students about the value of their day-to-day work in the classroom. One student remarked that the standardized test in his state was "just another hurdle I have to jump over in order to get to where I really want to go."

High stakes tests put pressure on students, parents, teachers, and administrators.

Teachers, also, feel the pressure of high stakes tests—like in Florida, for instance. Florida's Comprehensive Assessment Test (FCAT) is aligned with state standards and includes extended-response sections as well as multiple-choice items. However, this newly implemented test has teachers worried that they're going to have to abandon what they already know and believe about teaching in order to make sure that students achieve at high levels on the FCAT. A president of a local teacher's union in Florida stated that "all the teachers in my district believe that the curriculum has been wiped out by the test." Change is uncomfortable even for dedicated professionals who truly want the best for their students. States must implement all of the pieces of a standards reform package, including alignment of curriculum with standards and professional development in order for teachers to realize that standards and standardized tests support what they are doing with students instead of undermining it.

Enormous community and district pressure to raise test scores has driven some school personnel to use inappropriate methods to influence test scores. For example, as reported in an *Education Week* article entitled "As Expectations Rise, Definition of Cheating Blurs," a teacher in Reston, Virginia, was suspended for drilling students on questions that appeared on the state's social studies assessment. And in Woodland, California, several high school science teachers were suspended because they photocopied part of the high stakes exam, the Stanford Achievement Test, and taught the content that appeared on it.

In response to internal and external pressure, many administrators have begun to incorporate more test-prep materials, software, and strategies into the classroom. Robert Schaeffer, public education director of the National Center for Fair and Open Testing, explains the shift in the school district's approach in *Teacher Magazine*: "When superintendents, principals, teachers, and school boards are going to be judged on test scores, anyone who is surprised by the expansion of coaching in that direction is on a different planet" (Shea, 34). While the desirability of this trend is hotly debated throughout the educational arena, the collaboration with test-prep companies underscores the significance of these state tests.

In response to these and other opinions and incidents, some members of school communities have campaigned to halt the spread of high stakes tests. A group of parents spearheaded a campaign in Wisconsin to overturn the governor's efforts to institute a pass/fail high school graduation test. In Chicago, a group of high school students called Organized Students of Chicago drew up a petition that stated, "We are tired of excessive emphasis on standardized tests . . . Our schools do have problems, but they can only be solved by actually changing the way students are educated instead of simply giving more tests" (Rhodes, 41).

When what counts ultimately is a number, rather than the experience derived from both success and failure, the test can distract from the intrinsic value of learning.

When test scores, and not the test experience itself, are the focus, we take away from the intrinsic value of learning.

Schools with stellar scores reap congratulatory headlines, and schools that fall short earn the exposés, the articles that question what went wrong, and the interviews with panic-stricken realtors. As you read the papers, you begin to doubt and criticize, and are skeptical of the rationales the administrators deliver. People glibly pronounce judgments on the quality of education in the district based on the results of one test, and draw comparisons between districts based on those same numbers. By urging the public to take the tests very seriously, administrators may unwittingly create the perception that the test is the definition of the school system.

Alfie Kohn, an outspoken critic of standardized testing, predicts catastrophic results "if states persist in making a student's fate rest on a single test" (60). He argues that high standards are a cruel joke in the absence of resources and strategies to teach all students well. Instead of high stakes testing, Kohn states that "to take the cause of equity seriously is to work for the elimination of tracking, for more equitable funding, and for the universal implementation of more sophisticated approaches to pedagogy (as opposed to heavily scripted direct-instruction programs)" (47).

The state test should provide valuable information about your teenager's performance on state standards: "This is where I am, this is what I am good at, this is what I'm not good at." You are entitled to information about all aspects of the test. The questions on the following page are ones you should have the answers to, and they show that there is a lot to know about a standardized test. Standardized test scores can be incorrect because of errors in the test or scoring process. If your teen normally does well on tests yet receives a failing score, you should consider the possibility that the score is incorrect and question it with a school administrator. In chapters 4 and 5, we provide detailed information about how to communicate your concerns effectively to both teachers and administrators.

Questions to Guide Your Inquiry

- What does the state test measure?
- What is the difference between the state test and other tests?
- Who takes the test, and what is the timeline?
- How are the tests scored?
- How and when are scores reported?
- Will the state test affect my teenager's grade?
- How does the test impact district evaluations and graduation requirements?
- Are tests from previous years released to the public? Can I get access to them?
- Whom do I contact if I have additional questions?
- Why is the state undertaking this assessment program?
- How can a high school student do well on the SAT and not do well on the state test?
- Do these tests encourage teachers to "teach to the test"?
- Are these tests used or going to be used as high school graduation requirements?
- Can a school potentially lose accreditation because of poor performance on the test?
- What will be done to address the needs of students with disabilities?
- Can students retake the test?
- How often are the content areas of the test reviewed? Who conducts the review?
- What are the policies for transfer students who enter the state after the test has been administered?
- What is the appropriate procedure for questioning a test score?

In many states, individual school boards have the power to determine whether student test scores are used as a graduation requirement or as a criterion for promotion to the next grade level. If that is the case in your state, you can use the suggestions in chapters 4 and 5 to gather information from teachers and administrators that will help you build a case to present to the board of education. In other states, the department of education has specific policies that determine how test scores impact both the students and their respective school districts. In this case, the teachers and administrators in your district may be doing their best with a testing mandate they have had no hand in creating.

If you have done your research and are convinced that your state test has negatively impacted the quality of teaching and learning in your school district, you can advocate for change. In chapter 3 we describe in more detail how schools prepare for standardized assessments. You may find that your concerns are shared by teachers and administrators in your local district. Working together, you can better ensure that all pieces of a standards reform package are in place so that the state test supports rather than detracts from the work of all members of the school community.

Chapter at a Glance

The methods used to improve student performance by central administration, school administration, and classroom teachers will be explained and evaluated in this chapter. This information will help you understand how the school prepares for standardized testing.

Information

- The standardized test helps the school gather information about student performance.
- Administrators and teachers must work together to prepare students well for the standardized test.
- The central administration is responsible for informing the community about the standardized test and for determining how the district can best use the testing process and results.
- The school administration has to decide how to use available resources to train all staff members in the most efficient and productive way possible.
- Teachers need to incorporate key skills from the test into their daily lesson plans.
- The balance between teaching the test and teaching the curricula can become precarious.
- Standardized testing can refocus and strengthen public education.

How Schools Prepare for Standardized Tests

The state department of education releases scores for its standardized test and the news resounds like a thunderclap—in several locations. The Board of Education scraps the agenda for its regular meeting in order to grill school officials about the scores. Principals are called on the carpet and they, in turn, summon the department chairs. Teachers sweat the individual numbers because they indicate which students in whose classes failed to make the grade. The newspapers pillory the schools that fared poorly, real estate agents wring their hands, and parents vent their outrage. "Where do our tax dollars go?" you ask. "Why didn't they tell me what was going on?" You feel completely out of the loop. Not only do dismaying scores take you by surprise, but you are not even sure what to complain about: the ERG, the rubric, mastery level, standards, or all of the above. Come to think of it, you aren't entirely certain what an ERG or a rubric is. But just as you are doing, the schools are grappling with weighty issues, juggling the existing curricula with newly perceived needs for more and better strategies to improve student performance on the tests. It is a difficult balancing act.

COMMON GROUND FOR SCHOOL COMMUNITY

Administrators and teachers work as a team designated to come up with the game plan for boosting student performance on the standardized state tests. Administrators have the broadest role in instituting and implementing policy; teachers have the most direct and concrete impact on students. Educators in our particular district in Connecticut believe that students should be as prepared as possible for any type of assessment experience. Coaches may not like the conditions under which they have to play, but they do have to prepare the team for whatever challenges lie ahead of them. It is the school's duty to prepare students to take tests the way that coaches prepare team members to play a game. Gery Chico, president of the Chicago school board, agrees. Chico accepts tests as a fact of life, saying, "We want you to think outside the box; we don't want you to be a drone test taker. But we'd better have given you the knowledge and tools to succeed" (Rhodes, 43).

STRATEGIES EMPLOYED BY CENTRAL OFFICE

Central administration is an umbrella term for the superintendent, assistant superintendents, and subject area or grade-level coordinators who govern the school district. Central administration's first duty is to answer the question that has probably already occurred to you: Why does my student have to take this test? As one of our district administrators revealed, the role of central administration is to provide a real rationale for taking the test seriously.

The message that administration sends about the importance of preparation sets the tone for the entire district's approach to the test.

The superintendent and support staff publicize the district's programs through the media, informing you why the test is being given, how it will be scored, how the schools will prepare students, and how individual students in the district will be affected by the test results. What you already know about the testing requirements you probably read in the central administration press releases or publications mailed home. Nevertheless, you may have questions this publicity has not answered. Will my teenager need a qualifying score to graduate? What options are available if he or she does not qualify? How will the school provide remediation for students who must be retested (or who choose to be retested)? These are sensitive issues for you as your teenager's advocate—perhaps intimidating ones as well, if you are new to the vocabulary and concepts of standardized testing. Don't worry. Chapters 4 and 5 will help you go about getting answers to your questions, and the glossary in the back of the book is an easy reference guide to the often confusing terms bandied about in the educational arena.

The central administration really needs to know and understand the assessment. They will have to find ways to make it work to serve the district. The test is a given; therefore, how can we use it? What can we learn from it? What does the assessment tell us about student learning that can help enrich our curricula?

One of the first places to go for answers is your state board of education. They train teachers and administrators on how to conduct the assessment and how to help students to prepare for it. The training shows how the test was created, what types of questions it asks, and what types of responses are sought. Also, the training instructs teachers on how the test is scored and allows them to practice scoring written responses. The benefit is that the people who have to give the test not only understand it, but also can teach their colleagues how to help students be successful. The administration's support for the test and the test givers sets a tone of collaboration and joint responsibility throughout the entire school community.

STRATEGIES EMPLOYED BY THE PRINCIPAL

School building administration consists of principals, assistant principals, and department chairs. Principals share the responsibility to justify the test, not only to the local school board, but also to parents, students, and teachers. The principal has a full plate of responsibilities. On the one hand, he or she has to provide students with a rich and challenging curriculum every day. The public does not want to hear that the schools are suspending or shortchanging vital curriculum in order to teach to a test that takes one week of the school year. On the other hand, unlike the work students do every day, the test results will be published in the newspapers, seen and heard on television and radio, and discussed in Board of Education meetings and over coffee at Starbucks. Although the central office is ultimately responsible for interpreting the test results to the public, each principal will have to explain, defend, and justify how his or her school performed. When the test scores are high, or at least improved, the principal finds it easy to talk about the successful strategies that garnered the positive results. When the scores dip, and the district is outperformed by its neighbors, the principal had better be prepared with a lengthy list of what the schools did to help students get ready for the test. Also, two more urgent questions ultimately come up: How will you help students who did poorly the first time do better when they retake the test? How will you use the test results to improve instruction (and do better next year)?

Although the central office interprets the test results, it's the principal who will have to explain and defend his or her school's performance.

Usually long before the state test is given, the principal arranges for staff members to familiarize themselves with the test structure, format, and content. The state almost always releases testing materials from prior years and gives detailed descriptions of the test in the aforementioned training sessions. The principal has to decide how to use all this available information to train his or her staff members. It may be by encouraging meetings of teachers who teach the same subject or at the same grade level. Together, they discuss the test, trying to create consistent school-wide strategies to prepare students. You may worry that with the variety and diversity of teaching styles found in every school, your own teenager may be shortchanged and receive poor preparation. But although there will always be variables in instruction, teams of teachers working with consistent test-preparation strategies should put your worst fears to rest.

The principal may designate teacher leaders to manage preparation for a grade level or subject area. Usually these will be the teachers who have taken the most training and have the deepest and most positive interest in the testing program. Under the principal's leadership in our Connecticut district, teachers have taken the initiative to develop classroom activities that parallel the state assessments. Using them in the classroom teaches, strengthens, and reinforces the skills assessed by the standardized tests, and they remain in the district to be used as a resource.

A final but vital duty of the school principal is to manage the testing schedule. Although states are often rigid in setting rules for administering the tests (time of day, number of days, length of session, etc.), the principal has some latitude in setting up a schedule that preserves the integrity of the test while doing as little as possible to disrupt the day-to-day routine of learning. Standardized tests consume chunks of time when they are administered—in our state, Connecticut, it's the better part of two weeks. Attention paid to scheduling can minimize the disruption.

STRATEGIES EMPLOYED BY TEACHERS

The teacher's interest in increasing student performance seems self-evident: Teachers want to teach and they want students to learn. Naturally they welcome anything that gives their students the opportunity to demonstrate what they have learned.

But the picture for teachers is complex. Although they want test scores to improve, administrators and teachers must find a way to achieve this goal without sacrificing the content, skill, and personal development inspired by each subject area. They have an obligation to the curricula that they teach, and that, for most of them, represents a genuine deep interest. They love their subject and love to communicate that to students. Their students,

> *Teachers must find a way to improve test scores without sacrificing the content, skill, and personal development of the subject at hand.*

however, are a variable bunch. Every class, like every teenager, is unique, and curriculum needs to be tailored to the needs of the learners. Your experience with the differences among your own children illustrates the immensity of this job.

The addition of a mandatory standardized test at some point in the year has several results. It takes time from class to administer; it takes even more time to prepare students; it takes great effort to integrate the demands of the test with the structure and content of the existing curriculum. The newest component of the school year takes on even greater importance because it is so public. When the scores come out, individual teachers may feel threatened if their students did not perform as well as others. They are understandably worried about the impact of test preparation on their curriculum—perhaps even on their job security.

Teachers in our district believe that our state test is valuable. As one of our colleagues put it, "Preparing students for this test is just good teaching." On grade level and subject level, teachers discuss the test. What skills does it assess? What activities do we now use to teach or reinforce those skills? What do we need to incorporate into our curriculum to teach and reinforce them? How do we strike a balance, short-changing neither the existing curriculum nor the assessment? For example, in the literature portion of the Connecticut high school assessment exam (CAPT) students are asked to read a short story at the beginning of the 70-minute session. They then have the remainder of the time to answer four questions about their reading that measure a variety of higher-level thinking skills. In order to prepare students for the test, teachers use the same four questions when they read and write about literature on a daily basis in the classroom. The questions, or variations on them, are reasonable prompts to use when discussing literature, even when no state test looms in the future. Also, these teachers take pains to have students practice with the questions in a timed writing experience, for two reasons. First, the state test—and possibly other writing tests in general—will demand a timed writing; and second, learning to write under time pressure is a valuable skill.

Another way that we teachers try to prepare students is to give them a practice assessment in the same setting and with the same format. For example, when the tenth graders are actually taking the state assessment, the ninth graders take one, too. This way, the freshmen participate in a simulation of the test conditions, after which pairs of teachers can read and score the writing samples according to the guidelines provided by the state. The practice test informs teachers which of their students are succeeding and which are failing, and in specific areas. If the first and third questions, for example, gave students the most trouble, teachers can refocus instruction to reinforce the skills the students need to answer those questions more effectively. Feedback to students (and their parents) lets them know how they would probably score if they were to take the actual test, in hopes of giving them incentive to work harder on skill deficits and capitalize on skill strengths with further practice.

Administrators and teachers both endorse the concept of practicing for the test, focusing instruction on the skills necessary to prepare students to succeed at any and all assessments. Carefully thought-out practice has several advantages: It helps pre-pare students for how the test is administered, familiarizes them with the format, and allows them to practice meeting the standards they will need to succeed on the actual test. Some of the school-based activities that teachers have generated exhibit all these features and represent the best way to practice for a test.

Too much practice, however, can make both students and teachers anxious and produce more problems than benefits (see chapter 2). For example, in our district, elementary school students take state mastery tests in grades four, six, and eight. One value that is stressed in their language arts test is elaboration with details and examples in writing. A result of overpreparation for this test is that many students do not write succinctly when another assignment calls for a concise response, illustrating what goes wrong when we focus too hard on a single feature of a stan-dardized test.

Once the state test has been administered, the next step is for teachers to sit down with administrators to take a measured look at the scores, assess strengths and weaknesses, and collaborate on a plan to improve instruction. Treating the test as a learning experience for them-selves, too, can enrich curriculum. As they gain more practice at raising standards and communicating them to

Treating the test as a learning experience for both teachers and students enriches the curriculum.

students, the focus in the classroom sharpens and teachers are better prepared to suggest revisions to curriculum and undertake new approaches.

In the realm of standardized testing, the roles and strategies of central administrators, principals, and teachers are still evolving. When all members work together effectively, the test can make sense to students, blend with and not supplant curriculum, and increase student performance, not just on one task but consistently across the curriculum.

As a parent, your role in all this is not insignificant. The next two chapters focus on providing you with questions and ideas to clarify what the schools are trying to do and help you to enter the process as a participant more actively and confidently.

OPENING THE LINES OF COMMUNICATION

Chapter at a Glance

We will provide you with goals, protocols, and questions for your communication with teachers in this chapter. This information will help you become a confident, effective, and valued partner in the education of your teenager and help you reinforce the work of the school at home.

Information

- You are entitled to information from teachers about the material to be covered, assignments, how grades are determined, and what is being done to do to prepare your teenager for the standardized test.
- If you have a concern, start with a parent-teacher conference.

Action

- Advise teachers of the specific nature of your concerns ahead of time so that they can be prepared.
- If you are not satisfied with the information you have received, seek a meeting with a department representative before conferring with the principal.

How to Communicate with Teachers 4

As you linger outside the classroom door, you mentally review one more time what issues you want to address in the conference. Although you had to reschedule several other appointments to be here at 2:00 in the afternoon, you are pleased with yourself for following through and for being involved in your teenager's education. The door opens and you introduce yourself to the teacher. You slide into a desk and lead off with a comment about how much your child enjoys the class. The teacher begins to talk about a project that your daughter just finished and offers some interesting insights into the subject material as well as her performance. After about ten minutes, the teacher glances down at his watch and announces that another meeting is scheduled soon. "What can I do to help you?" You try to start a conversation about the state test and the teacher does his best to allay your fears. "Your child will do fine . . . We are working together to get ready for the exam . . . I don't think it is worth worrying about . . . Is there anything else I can do for you?" And with a handshake and a thank you, the meeting is over.

CORNERSTONES OF CONVERSATION

Before you attend a conference with a teacher, it is important to reflect on how you perceive your relationship with him or her. Do you regard the school staff member as a partner or a personal employee? Although this may sound like a loaded question, some teachers can feel patronized because of a parent's line of questioning during a meeting. You are entitled to accountability from teachers about what they have done and will continue to do to prepare your teenager for the state test. On the other hand, teachers want to be treated as professionals and supported by their communities.

Take time to speak with your teenager's teachers in the early months of the school year. These conversations will help you understand any specific instructional strategies they use to prepare students, and perhaps you will receive advice about how you can support their work in the classroom. Since it will take up to several months for the teachers to have a good grasp on your child's academic strengths and weaknesses, it is important to follow up periodically to see whether adjustments are needed.

When a conference is initiated by a teacher, there generally is a clear agenda that prompted the meeting, such as a disciplinary concern or academic opportunity. In these situations, the participants quickly get to the matter at hand and usually arrive at some resolution or next step within the allotted period of time.

When a conference is initiated by the parent, however, the agenda is not always as clear. A parent may explain to the teacher over the phone, "I want to talk about how my teenager is doing" or "I want to get more information about what is going on in class." These generalizations, however, can encompass any number of topics, and can leave the teacher in an uncomfortable position at the time of the conference. Be clear about why you have called for the conference. This gives both parties a chance to prepare for the discussion.

Additional Considerations

- Make the reason for the conference clear when you arrange the appointment.
- Bring your questions with you.
- If you don't understand the response, ask a clarifying or follow-up question.
- Ask to see sample resources, materials, and/or curriculum to illustrate the teacher's responses.
- Record the responses either during or immediately after the conversation.
- Arrange a follow-up meeting with the appropriate person to answer any additional questions and/or to receive a second opinion.

Questions for the Teacher

Conversations between teachers and parents on standardized testing will naturally evolve to include other topics related to your teenager's progress, personality, and academic standing. Although you have a specific goal, to get information on the preparation process for the test (see chapter 3), it also is essential to learn how that process is integrated into the curriculum and instruction in the course. This additional information not only will provide you with a more well-rounded understanding of the course, but also will help to put the standardized test into perspective. Remember, the test is just one indicator in a series of important indicators throughout the curriculum. Parents can and should ask a teacher for a complete overview of the material to be covered in the class, a list of the primary assignments with a schedule (test dates, project due dates), and information about how the student's grade will be determined.

Although teachers will likely be able to respond to your questions without advance notice, they may not be able to provide the level of specificity or relevant materials at that time. It often is a good idea to follow up with the teacher several days after the meeting to discuss future strategies, relevant information, and other ideas. The more focused your conversation can be the first time, the more likely you are to come out of that conversation with the information you need to be able to support your teenager's preparation for the standardized test.

The questions you prepare for your child's teacher should help you meet your goals for the conversation.

Additional Considerations

- Allow enough time. You will need at least 30 minutes for a thorough discussion of four to six questions.

- Stay focused on your goal. Try not to get sidetracked in discussions about other aspects of school life.

- Listen carefully. This initial conversation is for you to gain more information and insight.

- Ask to see sample exercises given to students to prepare them for the test so that you have a clearer understanding of both the preparation process and the test itself.

- Make sure you are speaking the same language. If the teacher uses terminology that you can't quite follow, ask questions until you understand.

A classroom teacher can offer very concrete suggestions about how to work with your teenager at home in preparation for the test. The principal, though, is the best person to ask about the school's overall vision for raising test scores or about the fluctuations in scores over the past five years. (Chapter 5 addresses how to communicate with your school's principal.)

Your questions should help you to meet your concrete and philosophical goals for the conversation. It is a good idea to write out your questions ahead of time and record the responses during or immediately after the meeting. Not only will this process save time, but it also will help you to reflect on areas where you may need additional information or a second opinion.

The following pages include sample questions to help focus your conversation with the teacher. If you feel comfortable doing so, it may help the teacher to see a copy of your questions beforehand. This gesture shows that you are genuinely interested in the preparation and administration process of the test, and it ensures that both of you are clear on the objectives of the conference.

Parent Questions	Teacher Responses
What strategies do you use to prepare students for the state test?	
How is my teenager doing so far in his or her efforts to meet the state standards?	
What can I do at home to help support my teenager in the test-preparation process?	
How closely do you think my teenager's grade on the test will match his or her grade in this class?	

Parent Questions	Teacher Responses
How are the state standards integrated into the curriculum for this class?	
How is preparation for the test integrated into the curriculum for this class?	
Were your test-preparation strategies provided by the state or developed locally?	
Are the scoring guidelines you use for test preparation available to students? To parents?	

GOING THROUGH APPROPRIATE CHANNELS

If you are uncomfortable with the strategies or approach of the teacher to the test, you should set up a follow-up meeting with a department chair, cluster leader, or teacher-leader to discuss the issue in more detail. At this point, it still is possible that you two had a miscommunication or that the teacher was vague because he or she did not know you wanted more precise details. The teacher may downplay the significance of the test because of personal feelings about the role of standardized tests, a desire not to alarm parents or students, professional flexibility in how to address the test in his or her classroom, or a lack of specific knowledge about the test. Continue to be positive, but be firm that you want more information about how the state standards are incorporated into the curriculum and how students are prepared for the test.

If this meeting proves to be unsuccessful, the next step is a meeting with the school principal (see chapter 5). This step not only indicates your seriousness about the issue, but also becomes a school personnel issue as well. Because the principal was not involved in the earlier meetings, it is important to provide details about those meetings in a calm and rational manner. Provide the details in written form in advance of the meeting so that the principal knows where you are coming from and what you are looking for. This pre-conference communication also will give the principal a chance to meet with any other teachers involved to listen to their perspectives on the meetings.

You can also approach your district administrator and/or board of education. The focus of the next chapter is on how to communicate with administrators about what is being done on the building and district levels to achieve better standardized test scores as well as improve the quality of teaching and instruction. If you disagree with the policy or position of the school, you can discuss these issues on the district level as well, but you should engage in this debate on the principles rather than on the individual personalities involved. Remember that the goal is to help your teenager prepare for the state test, not to create a war at school. The purpose of these conversations is to understand how you are working together in order to help that happen.

Chapter at a Glance

In this chapter you'll find goals, protocols, and questions for your communication with administrators. This information will help you become a confident, effective, and valued participant in the discussion of how to prepare students for standardized tests.

Information

- You are entitled to accountability from administrators about what they have done and will continue to do to improve the quality of education.

Action

- Ask for information about the standardized test when your teenager begins high school and again early in the year when the test is administered.
- Request clarification of language or statistics that you don't understand.
- Look for ways to learn more about standards and standardized state tests by participating in a curriculum review committee or school improvement group.

How to Communicate with Administrators 5

As you wait in the school office, you gaze at the students and staff who race by. There is an electric mix of energy, confidence, and youth in the air that tugs your mind back to the days when you walked the halls of high school. You wonder if your teenager encounters the same highs and lows that exalted and troubled your adolescent years. A figure in front of you motions you back into the present: "The principal will see you now." After a smile and a firm handshake, the principal motions for you to take a seat at the round table in her office and then asks what she can do to help you. You have stuffed envelopes, supported fund-raisers, baked, chauffeured, and attended sporting and musical events regularly and faithfully. Yet your role in the development of standards and state tests has been marginal at best. You have never been in on the planning stages. You are a little suspicious of what schools are doing in the areas of educational reform. The questions, the concerns, the ideas, and the blood come rushing to your brain all at the same time. You think, the more things change, the more they stay the same. And then you begin to speak.

SITTING DOWN AT THE TABLE

It is important to emphasize that you are entitled to information from your local school administrators about the testing process. Although you do have this right and should be encouraged to exercise it, you should choose your time and strategies carefully in order to effectively communicate with the school. Before striking up a conversation with school personnel, first determine your goals. On a philosophical level, you probably are in search of sane and reasonable accountability. In his renowned book *Results: The Key to Continuous School Improvement*, Dr. Mike Schmoker—a firm believer that all school efforts should be focused on results—

writes, "Parents, communities, and local employers want to know not only about a school and its programs but also how well the school is doing" (47). In other words, he says, what do we want for our children, and how do we know if we're getting it?

Your concern may stem not just from your own teenager's scores, but from a perceived weakness in the overall academic experience provoked by comparatively low school rankings. You may have read the local newspaper and been unpleasantly surprised by the overall performance of your teenager's school.

Although it is only natural to be interested in the ranking of your school district in comparison to local area towns, the days immediately following the public release of the scores may not be the most productive time to sit down with school officials. A *New York Times* article published in June 2000 illustrated perfectly the rash and sometimes distorted reaction of many suburban parents to published test scores.

Scores for the Regents, the New York state reading and writing tests, were released by school and district in newspapers statewide, setting off horror and fury in some suburban schools as scores came in far lower than expected. Several superintendents and principals held meetings where they found themselves reasoning with angry parents—often to little avail—that the tests were still in the trial phase, that the scores were a baseline, not a judgment. It is not as if these schools did poorly; the anger came in districts where more than 80 percent of students passed. But here, the issue is not whether schools pass, it is how well they do, and how much better they do than other schools. The author of the article then went on to interview a real estate broker who reports that her clients use standardized test scores "like the Bible to decide where they're going to live" (B2).

It is important to keep in mind that while standardized tests can serve as an important indicator of student performance, the vast majority of education professionals would argue that these tests are only one of a number of valid indicators of overall student learning. In fact, in some states the tests have higher stakes for the school district than for the individual students and their families. Students' scores on the Kansas Assessment Program (KAP), for example, are used for school accreditation and school performance reporting in that state.

> *Most education professionals believe that state standardized tests are only one of a number of valid indicators of student learning.*

BEGINNING THE CONVERSATION

When your teenager enters the school, you should consider sitting down at the table with school administrators to address the more philosophical questions of how state standards have been incorporated into curricula and how students are prepared for the test. Why approach a school administrator for this conversation? Because his or her job responsibilities likely include the coordination of test preparation, oversight of curriculum and professional development, and/or accountability for teacher evaluations. These global and serious responsibilities provide administrators with unique insight into the learning process for students throughout their time in the school. Although teachers also can offer important insights into these philosophical inquiries, their responses are more localized based on their own classroom experiences.

You can obtain the schedule for administration of standardized tests from the school district's central office; you can also conduct your own research on your state department of education's Website (see chapter 2 for more details).

GOING THROUGH APPROPRIATE CHANNELS

Your first resource for information should be administrators within the school your child attends. On the department level, there is typically a coordinator or chairperson for each subject area. Depending on the size of the school, building administration may consist solely of the principal or may include one or more assistant principals as well. Each of these administrators may have different areas of specialization. Make it clear that you are seeking information about standardized testing when you request an appointment.

Additional Considerations

- Allow enough time. You will need at least 30 minutes for a thorough discussion of four to six questions.

- Stay focused on your goal. Try not to get sidetracked in discussions about other aspects of school life.

- Listen carefully. This initial conversation is for you to gain more information and insight.

- Make sure you are speaking the same language. If the administrator uses terminology or points to statistical trends that you can't quite follow, ask questions until you understand.

- Be positive and supportive. Unfortunately, administrators are used to "handling" parents and community members who have hidden agendas.

- Ask about opportunities to participate in group discussions about standards and testing. Most schools have curriculum review committees, site-based improvement teams, and/or community discussion groups that meet at least several times a year.

The following pages include sample questions to help focus your conversation with the administrator. If you feel comfortable doing so, it may help the administrator to see a copy of your questions beforehand. Not only does this gesture show that you are genuinely interested in the preparation and administration process of the test, but it also ensures that both of you are clear on the objectives of the conference.

Parent Questions	Administrator Responses
How will my teenager's test results impact his or her academic standing?	
What methods of communication does the school use to inform parents about the state test, preparation, administration, and results?	
What testing accommodations are available for special-needs students?	
Are there specific courses that my teenager should take in order to be better prepared for the test?	

Parent Questions	Administrator Responses
What can I do to support the work of the school in this area?	
How do administrators ensure that each curriculum is aligned with state standards for that content area?	
Are parents invited to participate in curriculum revision and/or professional development experiences related to standards and state tests?	
What is the school's policy on curriculum revision?	
What professional development opportunities and resources are available to help teachers and administrators keep up with changes to the state standards and tests?	

After the conference, spend some time to record and reflect upon the responses. It is important that your new information is consistent with the information you have received from the state department of education as well as from other personnel in the school district.

If, upon reflection, you have serious concerns about the school-based efforts to prepare students for the assessment, it is appropriate to ask for a meeting with the district administrator responsible for curriculum, assessment, and instruction. The title of this administrator will vary depending upon the size of your school district. The questions on the preceding pages for the principal or other building-level administrator responses also are quite apt here. Keep in mind that the source of your concerns may be due to miscommunication with the administrator you speak with rather than significant flaws in the strategies employed by the high school staff. Continue to listen carefully to the district administrator's overview of the philosophy and process adopted and ask clarifying questions where needed.

Administrators and parents alike want to see students be more successful, and that common ground should be a positive place to work from in the conversation. You can engage in especially meaningful and effective conversations with school administrators when you establish a consistent relationship throughout the school year. Support your teenager and the school as a whole through participation in activities. Not only does your involvement in a booster club, parent teacher association, curriculum review committee, or classroom generate immediate respect for your investment in school life, but it also increases your potential influence because of your ability to network with other parents involved in the activities.

Your support of and involvement in your teenager's school generates respect and increases your potential influence.

In addition to these benefits, your involvement reinforces to your teenager that you are invested in his or her life and interests. Keeping an open line of communication with your child is certainly of utmost importance, especially during the turbulent teenage years. In chapter 6 we focus on how you can more effectively communicate with your teen about school. From research data to common experience, it is overwhelmingly clear that parents can have a dramatic impact on the personal and academic success of high school students.

Chapter at a Glance

This chapter will explain ways that you can support the work of the schools at home. This information will help you contribute to the quality of your teen's academic experience.

Information

- Even though we want schools to do a better job of teaching, both parents and teachers are reluctant to abandon traditional conceptions of teaching and learning.
- There are different types of intelligence that have a significant impact on how students learn.

Action

- Talk with your teenager about his or her day so you can be a sounding board for problems and a supportive ear to listen to good and bad news.
- Get into the habit of saving your teenager's work both to supplement portfolio development at school and to underscore the value of his or her academic accomplishments.
- Discuss with teachers what type of learner your teenager is so that you and they can provide more meaningful support in the learning process.

How to Communicate with Your Teen 6

It's the end of a long day. You're tired and ready for some well-earned downtime. You're trying to decide whether to have a cup of coffee, go for a walk, or get a drink from the fridge. But, first, you want to check in with your son. You knock on his bedroom door but he doesn't hear you because he's got Sugar Ray's "Personal Space Invader" on full blast. "Two steps back, you're in my space," booms from behind the closed door. You knock louder, maybe a little louder than you meant to. Your son clicks off the CD player. "Yeah?" he says. "I just wanted to say hi," you reply pleasantly. "What?" he shouts. You open the door and poke your head in. "I just wanted . . . " you begin. "What ever happened to knocking?" he inquires, eyes still glued to the computer monitor. You start to say, "I DID knock," but, instead, you take a very deep breath.

As the air moves into your lungs, time seems to stop, and you face one of a parent's biggest dilemmas: Will you be human or heroic? Will you ask if he's done his homework, accept his yes, close the door, and seek immediate downtime? Or will you ask him to turn the CD back on so you can hear the rest of the song because it's kind of interesting? And once you've talked about the song lyrics a bit, maybe you'll ask if his English teacher's made any off-the-wall assignments recently. And then you'll get around to what he's working on, which may be a difficult level in his new computer game, but which may, with superhuman patience, careful listening, and some adroit segues, lead to a discussion of his work at school that is open and comfortable for you both. Maybe.

STAYING IN TOUCH

So what does the weary parent do? Compromise. Say something that is both welcoming and honest and that gives you a chance to catch your breath: "Hi, I'd like to hear the rest of that song but I need a couple of minutes to decompress." Use whatever strategy works for you to release the day's tension and then return to your teenager's lair. Listen to the CD or watch the video, TV program, or computer game for a few minutes. Ask questions, make comments. Talk a little bit about your day, including problems and frustrations that you faced. Teenagers have a way of listening without appearing to. By this time, "How was your day?" might get a response, one that might be elaborated on.

And here's where knowledge of the standards movement pays off. The parent who is familiar with school and state standards (see chapters 1 and 2) knows that part of the point of these standards is to encourage students to respond, to make connections, to evaluate, to reflect—in short, to experience and articulate feelings and thoughts about the world and its diverse inhabitants and artifacts. With any luck, discussion of the day will include some mention of schoolwork. If it doesn't, ask about just one course, the one your

Part of the point of state standards is to encourage students to respond, make connections, evaluate, and reflect.

teenager tends to like the most and to speak about most easily. You can follow up on "So what are you working on in _____?" with a few questions that invite your teenager to share good news and to use you as a sounding board for problems.

Suggested Questions

- How's it going?
- Where did you come up with your idea?
- What have you learned so far?
- Have you run into any problems?
- Are you getting feedback from your teacher? Other students? Would you like some feedback from me?
- Have you been able to help anyone else?
- What are other students doing with this assignment?
- What's easy about this? What's hard?
- Is there anything you need in the way of materials or resources that I can help you get? When do you need them?
- What connections have you been able to make with what you already know?
- What else would you like to know?
- How will you make sure that your ideas are understood by your teacher? Other students?
- What are the requirements for the format?
- Do you have to turn in documentation of your process or just a final product?
- What have you learned about yourself by doing this?

Another way that you can support your teenager's efforts is to treat his or her work as a valuable artifact that requires respectful storage. Many schools are using portfolios in various ways. Sometimes this is an ongoing collection of the student's work, which means that work may remain in a folder at school. Other times, especially with older students, work will be sent home with the expectation that the student will save it to make a reflective portfolio at the end of the semester or year. These days, portfolio construction is just as likely to happen in math or science as it is in language arts or social studies. A word of caution: Saving work on the hard drive of a computer may not be enough, for two reasons. Some teachers want documentation of process in the portfolio, so the student will need to produce a sequence of drafts with comments and revisions. Also, your hard drive may crash at some point during the year, erasing all records of the student's work. Encourage your teenager to save everything to a backup disk, as well as to the hard drive, and offer your services as curator for his or her collected works.

Learn How Your Teen Learns

On a more theoretical level, you can increase learning and reduce frustration by showing sensitivity to the unique mix of strengths and weaknesses that shape the way your teenager perceives the world and operates in it. Literally dozens of different types of intelligence have been identified by researchers, the best known of whom is Howard Gardner. However, as Carol Ann Tomlinson points out in

> *Be sensitive to the unique way your teen perceives the world and operates in it.*

The Differentiated Classroom, "While the names of intelligences vary, educators, psychologists, and researchers have drawn two significant, consistent conclusions:

- People think, learn, and create in different ways.
- Development of our potential is affected by the match between what we learn and how we learn with our particular intelligences" (18).

Although there are many valid ways to categorize intelligence and learning preferences, we believe that awareness of three learner profiles will be especially helpful to parents. As we teachers get to know our students, we gain an understanding of what makes each one of them unique and of the characteristics they share with students we've taught in the past. These three learner profiles are based on those shared characteristics.

Often, expectations about learning on the part of both parents and teachers revolve around one specific kind of learner. This learner fits the image of a studious young man or woman, illuminated by a pool of lamp light, head bent diligently over a hefty textbook. This is a *classic learner*, one who readily soaks up information from the printed word, and who processes information best in a quiet atmosphere, sitting at a well-lit desk. The image of the lamp is a metaphor for the respect in which we tend to hold this type of learner. Much of the work that goes on in high school is geared towards students whose strengths are in these areas. However, this type of learner tends to need help in making the leaps that result in intellectual or emotional insights and may be deficient in "people" skills.

Understand and accommodate your teenager's learning profile.

Social learners, on the other hand, want to spread out their work at ground zero of family life and talk it over with someone. Silence and solitude make these learners feel restless and unfocused. Social learners are no less competent than classic learners; they just need to articulate facts and ideas in conversation with another human in order to make them personal and, therefore, memorable. Their attempts to learn are often met with misunderstanding, because parents hoping for classic learner behaviors see these attempts to create meaningful connections between life and learning as attempts to procrastinate.

Conscientious parents are probably most frustrated with *divergent learners*, as they appear to be doing anything but homework. As youngsters, these learners are likely to be found sitting on a chair or couch upside down. Draped over furniture, divergent learners tend to multitask. They simultaneously doodle, listen to music, watch TV, talk on the phone, *and* do homework. These learners tend to make insightful connections and solve problems in unexpected ways. However, if your teenager is a divergent learner, he or she may occasionally run into difficulty by going off on a tangent that is intrinsically interesting and justifiable, but does not, from the teacher's perspective, fulfill the assignment.

None of these learners is lacking in intelligence. They will all get it done if they are allowed make use of their strengths and receive understanding support in overcoming their weaknesses. Teachers, especially those who have recently entered the profession, receive training in meeting the needs of diverse learners. Nevertheless, in spite of this training and with the best intentions in the world, teachers, in particular high school teachers, tend to be classic learners themselves and their expectations may inadvertently favor this kind of learner.

It may be extremely helpful to meet with your teen's teachers to discuss these issues. These conversations will provide you with additional insight into what type of learner your child is, and can help you offer him or her more meaningful support. Although the concept of multiple intelligences has been around for years, only recently have teachers across the nation begun to focus on the issue as a serious consideration in curriculum and instructional design. Not only will you learn a lot from listening to your teenager's teachers, but you also will be able to further their understanding about how your child functions and what parameters are necessary for him or her to be successful.

Just as your teen's approach to learning may present a challenge to his or her teachers, it may be tough for you to accept an approach that is different from your own. Your teen needs to know that your expectations are high and that you see him or her as an individual capable of, say, loving math even though you hated it, or of doing homework with the CD player on full blast even though your own approach to learning requires quiet. You send a strong message to your teen through your casual comments about school and homework. A conscious effort to give these comments a positive spin will help your teen deal with the inevitable frustrations of adolescence. Listen, ask constructive questions, be open to your teen's way of doing things.

In the context of the high stakes tests that your teenager will almost certainly take, your understanding of him or her as learner will both facilitate and enrich the dialogue between parents and the schools when you sit down to discuss the test. Not only will your conversations in this area empower you to support your own teen, but you also will be able to communicate more effectively with other parents. Chapter 7 outlines different ways of networking, educating, and organizing with other parents to solidify the knowledge base about standardized state tests in your district.

Chapter at a Glance

Learn the ways that you can become involved in the standards and assessment movement in this chapter. This information will help you contribute to the conversation and education process in order to benefit your teenager as well as other members of the school community.

Information

- The traditional high school model can be counterproductive to student learning.
- The standards movement has helped to open a nationwide discussion about what high school students should know and be able to do.
- Parental involvement is essential if we are to realize the full potential of the standards movement.

Action

- Parents who receive encouragement and training to become involved in standards work can make significant contributions to the school and community.

How to Communicate with Other Parents

Imagine the ideal learning environment for your teenager. Does it include sitting at a desk for 43 minutes and then, at the sound of a bell, slamming a notebook into a backpack bursting at the seams, weaving a path through a corridor crowded with other adolescents, accidentally bumping into a large senior who yells, "Watch where you're going, you _____," slipping into a heavily carved desk-chair unit, reaching for yet another notebook, and repeating this performance five or six times every weekday from September to June? In the ideal environment, the halls would be less crowded, for starters. You wish that schools were doing more to teach kids to be nicer to each other, and you've wondered if your teenager really needs to study six or seven different subjects every day. You ponder the fact that your daughter seems to see learning as a chore now when she used to love counting games, nursery rhymes, and snuggling next to you to read. You worry that what she is studying at school is not completely compatible with what you teach at home. But you say to your-self, "Hey, high school has always been like this, so it must be okay. Right?"

IMPACT OF PARENTAL EXPECTATIONS ON HIGH SCHOOL

Certain characteristics of high school may indeed remain the same, but is this all right? Yes and no. Education theorists who have studied the natural patterns of teaching and learning that occur at home see these patterns as models that schools should emulate. In *Whole Earth Review*, John Gatto, veteran teacher and social critic, reminds us that "in the growth of human society, families came first, communities second, and only much later the institutions set up by the community to serve it" (60). As you become more informed and involved in standards and assessment, you will be in a position to advocate standards and strategies that align teaching and learning practices at school more closely with those of the families and communities schools are intended to serve.

The research indicates that the traditional high school is indeed "okay" for high-achieving students who have a lot of support from home, but it would be even better if high schools were smaller and there was more emphasis on essential questions and student-led inquiry. For students who lack motivation and support, the traditional high school can be so demeaning that it becomes counterproductive, making students actively resist learning.

In a June 2000 article for *Education Week* called "Between Hope and Despair," education consultants Tom Vander Ark and Tony Wagner identify an ironic barrier to change. "The public wants schools to be better, but not different. Our collective and idealized memory of high school may be the greatest impediment that we face" (50). But changing the model on which high school is based is easier said than done. There are some powerful assumptions behind the traditional high school that have sustained its use for fifty years and that are deeply ingrained in how we think about high school. Consider these:

- High school students must be taught by specialists in each academic discipline.
- The most efficient way to deliver specialized knowledge and skills is in a consolidated, comprehensive high school.
- Equity is achieved by delivering the same material to each student in the same way. (See "A Brief History of High School" at the back of this book.)

Everything that we associate with high school has evolved from these assumptions. Providing a high school education to every teenager in America is one of the most idealistic and ambitious social enterprises ever undertaken; however, the changes in American society over the last half century have been so sweeping that it is time to question these assumptions. We now live in an age of infinite information, unlimited access, and vanishing boundaries. The distinctions between math and science, foreign language and social studies, and language arts and business that must have seemed so clear fifty years ago are fading. We teachers must face the fact that it is impossible for any one

> *The assumptions behind the "traditional high school" are deeply ingrained in how we think about high school; however, the sweeping changes in American society force us to question these assumptions.*

of us to know everything about anything. Once we admit that we can't cover every-thing, we have to decide what knowledge and skills will be most meaningful to our students. And what will be meaningful to our students may not be what we, as parents and teachers, already know.

The standards movement has helped to open a nationwide discussion about what high school students should know. Instead of 43 minutes each of math, science, social studies, and language arts, think about what it would be like for your teenager to learn about all of these things in the context of a sustained, meaningful experi-ence—immersing themselves in a world language, managing an enterprise, teaching in an elementary school, planning and completing a long-term ecology project, participating in all facets of a performance art, and so on.

Large schools may be the best provider of opportunity, but problems, like anonymity among students, can arise.

Providing students with these varied learning opportunities, of course, is often highly correlative with the size of the school itself. Consolidation still makes sense in terms of both physical and human resources. Large schools provide materials and experiences that are beyond the means of small ones. However, problems arise when the popula-tion of the school becomes so large that individuals within it feel anonymous.

Adolescents are especially vulnerable to this phenomenon. The young person between 13 and 18 years of age who feels anonymous may experience depression so profound that it leads to dysfunction in all aspects of life and creates a potential for suicide. Another consequence of housing large numbers of adolescents together is an increased likelihood of crowd behavior. Adolescents are passionate and short-sighted. They need to test societal limits and experiment with various ways of defining themselves. The larger the student population, the more likely it is that these needs will result in spontaneous events that are damaging to individuals, property, and school climate. And the larger the student population, the harder it is for adults to provide guidance and for individuals to follow their ethical compass in opposition to the magnetism of the crowd.

Research indicates that schools are most effective when students experience a strong sense of belonging. Within the large school, each student needs a comfortable niche. You can help meet this need by working with your teenager at home, supporting extracurricular activities, and being open to alternatives to the traditional high school. As a parent aware of the issues, you can play an essential role in shaping the high schools of the 21st century.

THE ROLE OF PARENTS IN 21ST CENTURY SCHOOLS

Central to the standards movement is the recognition that assessment should not be a mysterious process through which students receive grades without understanding what they have done poorly or what they have done well. The purpose of standards is to share information that will help students make deliberate progress towards achievement at high levels (see chapter 1). Clearly, standards need to be shared with parents as well as with students. But this should not be a one-way delivery of information. A recent *Time* magazine article reported on a Nickelodeon/TIME poll of students, parents, and teachers that was conducted by Penn, Shoen, & Berland. The poll shows that high school students do benefit from parental interest and involvement in schoolwork. As discussed in chapter 6, parents who have gone to the trouble of becoming knowledgeable about standards and assessment will be better able to fulfill their child's continuing need for support.

A recent Public Agenda telephone interview showed that 55 percent of respondents saw the need for increased parental involvement as the major issue in contemporary education. In her commentary for *Education Week*, writer and public school parent Holly Holland confirms that studies conducted over the last 30 years have overwhelmingly shown that an involved and informed parent is a major determiner of a student's progress in school. Dozens of public opinion polls and surveys resoundingly confirm that parents are an essential component of effective education. Key findings of the study called "Strong Families, Strong Schools" include the fact that what the family does has far

> *Today's education needs more parental involvement.*

more impact on student achievement than socioeconomic status or the level of education reached by the parents. In addition, this study reveals that one of the greatest obstacles in the path of parental involvement in schools is not knowledge or ability but insecurity on the part of both parents and teachers. People who didn't experience a strong sense of belonging when they were in high school themselves are less inclined to return as parents.

Few teacher preparation programs include training in how to encourage parental involvement. The 1999 Public Agenda Survey called "Playing Their Parts" (which is available online at www.publicagenda.org) asked parents and teachers what role parents should be playing in public schools. One of their findings was especially interesting: "Many reform efforts focus on giving parents real power over hiring, curriculum, and budgets in public schools. We found few parents eager to take on that responsibility. Most parents felt they were ill prepared to make policy decisions, and most teachers agreed. However, [emphasis ours] *the teachers . . . who had participated in experiments giving parents more authority favored the idea.*"

Information, Please!

Joan Dykstra and Arnold Fege are parent activists who see a serious disconnect between education policymakers and parents. In their *Education Week on the Web* article (www.edweek.org), they point out that parents have been left out of the loop on standards development yet are asked to blindly accept standards and standards-based tests. "How is it possible," they ask, "to implement 21st century standards with 20th century models of citizen and parent participation?" Dykstra and Fege comment dryly that "a summit where governors and business leaders were not the major players, but where parents and other community members received the spotlight, would have been refreshing indeed."

Most of you would probably agree with that sentiment. The parents who met with us in June to talk about this book had quite a bit to say about how little they really know about standards and state tests. They told us about mixed messages and misinformation they had received. One parent summed it up when she said, "Parents of high school students believe that it is the school's responsibility to prepare students for state tests. If you want parents to embrace the value of the test, you have to start much earlier educating them about that value." Similarly, parents can't be expected to support standards when no one has bothered to tell them who is writing them or what they are supposed to accomplish. As Dykstra and Fege concluded, "the public must be a full partner to the dreams and visions education policymakers have for America's children."

In order to become full partners, parents must have access to information about standards and standards-based tests, an opportunity to participate in their development, and a clearly defined role in their implementation. Historically, parents have not been granted these things. You must go out and create them for yourselves.

GETTING THE WORD OUT

One way to gain the necessary access, opportunity, and defined role is to participate in teacher or parent-led workshops and discussion groups. Working as individuals, parents can learn the language of standards and assessments, investigate what their schools are already doing, and engage in conversation with educators. But to overcome long-standing assumptions (both their own and educators') that parents are not qualified to participate in decisions regarding standards and testing, they need to enlist other parents to amplify their voices. Discussion groups and workshops are simply informal meetings where parents can share what they already know, raise the issues that interest them, help other parents become informed, and develop strategies for future conversations with educators. The strength that develops when parents network with each other prepares them to become full partners in the goals and policies of their children's education.

With a handful of practical strategies, you can facilitate or create workshops and discussion groups to help other parents learn about standards and state tests. Let's use a sample parent workshop on reading standards to illustrate the following six key steps to help get the word out:

Step 1: Inclusion   **Step 4: Homework**

Step 2: Limits   **Step 5: Follow-up**

Step 3: Balance   **Step 6: Growth**

The approach taken for the reading standards workshop provides you with a useful starting point for designing a workshop on any topic. Once you have identified the content area that the workshop will address, visit your state department of education's Website to locate standards for that section of the test as well as sample test items. Many of these sites not only offer field-tested items and/or previous tests, but also cross-reference each item with

The goal is to get as many parents involved as possible.

the related state goal, indicator, or rubric to indicate how students will be tested. If this information is not readily available or easy to work with, contact your district's central office for these documents.

When you have a clear picture of what students are expected to know and be able to do, you will be in a better position to identify and appreciate the connection between local teaching methods and state tests. In addition, you can be more proactive as a member of school curriculum development committees, as an advocate during teacher-parent conferences, and as a consultant for your child on homework assignments.

Step 1: Inclusion

Invite everyone. Send a flyer home with students, put an announcement in the PTA newsletter or the local newspaper, advertise the meeting on local access television, send a letter to parents via first class mail—just get the word out. Typically, only one to two percent of those invited will actually show up for a workshop. However, the invitation itself, even if it is not accepted, is a way of disseminating information and getting parents to think about the issues.

DON'T MISS THIS WORKSHOP

What parents need to know about standards

Thursday, September 30th, 7:00 to 8:30 P.M., Room 239

Research shows that the amount of information parents have about academic expectations has a significant impact on student achievement. This workshop will provide an overview of the academic standards recently adopted by our State Department of Education:

- What's the purpose of standards?

- What's the difference between content and performance standards?

- What impact will standards have on my teen's program of study?

- How does parental awareness of standards increase student achievement on standardized tests?

ALL ARE WELCOME

Step 2: Limits

Offer the workshop on a day and time when you are least likely to interfere with family life and other school events. Typically a school secretary keeps an activities calendar that can be consulted in order to avoid conflicts and to reserve space in the building. Focus the workshop on one specific issue. One and a half hours is enough time to provide useful information and carry out meaningful activities.

- Give participants an agenda as they enter.
- Start on time.
- Defer big questions until the discussion period towards the end of the workshop.

The goal of the workshop is not just to let parents air their concerns about their own teenager's experience in school, but to give participants the information and confidence they need to become an effective part of the educational community.

The Home Front
What Parents Need to Know about Standards

7:00—Welcome and introduction (5 minutes)

The standards describe learning goals for all students in all subject areas, and provide indicators of what it looks like when students have met these goals. From the standards students can learn what is expected, and parents can receive guidance on how to support learning at home.

7:05—Overview of sample standards on reading (10 minutes)

Embedded in these standards are important concepts about education: for example, the value of learning a variety of strategies for reading and the importance of finding a personal connection to the reading. These concepts can best be understood by actually doing some reading together and then comparing what we've done with the standards.

7:15—A shared reading experience (45 minutes)

- Read aloud a short poem about parents and teens.
- Write a personal response.
- Read the poem again and list what we have learned from it.
- Discuss what makes a poem good and whether or not this is a good poem.
- Discuss the strategies we used to understand and evaluate the poem.
- Write a poem about your own teenager.
- Read through the standards and check the ones we used in our work with this poem.

8:00—Questions and discussion (25 minutes)

8:25—Orientation to strategies parents can use at home (5 minutes)

Step 3: Balance

Parents have different learning styles, just as students do. Back up information that is presented orally with banners, posters, and photographs or video clips of students that illustrate the issue under discussion. Organize hands-on activities in small groups so participants may share and discuss their work without having to take the risk of presenting it to everyone. Provide discussion time for those parents who are comfortable speaking to a larger group. If you have invited teachers and administrators to the workshop, make sure that the voices of both parents and educators are heard.

Step 4: Homework

The shared experience of the workshop will create a sense of belonging in the participants. Reinforce this perception with "homework" that will help them continue thinking about the issue and give them strategies to put their ideas into action at home.

Strategies for Parents

Think of your teenager as a reader (no matter how little he or she seems to read).

- Count magazines, e-mail, and Web surfing as reading.
- Express interest in where and when your teenager likes to read and help out with a cushion, a special bookmark, or a reading light.
- Encourage your teenager to read aloud to younger siblings or to you.
- Give books, bookstore certificates, and magazine subscriptions as gifts.

Share your own experiences as a reader.

- Explain how you select what you read.
- Recall a time when something you read touched you or changed your opinion.
- Describe strategies you've used to grapple with a difficult reading.
- Read passages aloud from your own reading materials and invite discussion.

Network to find appropriate magazines and books.

- Ask your teenager's friends what they are reading.
- Ask the high school and town librarians for lists of books geared to specific interests.
- Include discussion of what you're reading in conversations with family and friends.
- Consider joining or starting a book discussion club.

Make reading a family activity.

- Subscribe to a newspaper and a couple of journals related to family interests.
- Bring an audio book or something to read aloud on long car trips.
- Request books as gifts as well as giving books.
- Play games that involve language (Balderdash™, Scrabble™, Quiddler™, etc.).

Step 5: Follow-Up

Intensify each participant's sense of belonging and continue to disseminate information by sending out a follow-up survey. The results of the survey could serve as
the foundation for a discussion group or a newsletter. Don't be disappointed if
relatively few surveys are actually returned. The main purpose of the survey is to
remind parents about what they can do at home. Photocopy on the reverse side the
address to which the survey is to be returned so they can simply fold, staple, stamp,
and drop it in the mail.

The Home Front
What Parents Need to Know about Standards

Follow-Up Survey

Thank you for the pleasant evening we spent together talking about standards and reading and discussing a poem. Please take a few minutes to respond to the survey questions that follow by checking the statements that apply to you and your family.

❑ Made a positive comment about teenager's reading.

❑ Expressed interest in where and when teenager likes to read.

❑ Offered a small gift related to reading.

❑ Encouraged teenager to read aloud.

❑ Shared experiences as a reader.

❑ Read aloud to teenager.

❑ Invited discussion of a shared reading.

❑ Shared ideas with other parents.

❑ Discussed reading with family or friends.

❑ Participated in a book discussion club.

❑ Made a specific reference to the reading standards in conversation with teenager.

Step 6: Growth

Once the organizers and participants have demonstrated that parents can teach parents about standards, some options will open. If the workshop was initially offered as a PTA activity, follow-up can be integrated into the agendas for subsequent meetings, or a subcommittee can be formed for further study, additional workshops, and so on. If the workshop was offered independent of the PTA, participants can, of course, continue to hold workshops independently. However, once the word gets out, a reprise of the workshop is likely to be requested as a PTA activity, paving the way for integration of the independent work on standards into the established organization. Either way, the goal is to get as many parents involved as possible.

Informal discussion groups are another way to get the word out. Use the same strategies you used for the workshops in order to make the discussion groups inclusive, accessible, and meaningful for all participants. Even though the format is informal, discussion groups need an agenda that states a specific topic. Equally important is a facilitator who will cordially but firmly keep the discussion focused on that topic. Follow-up on a discussion group should include an invitation for parents to suggest topics for further discussion.

Possible Discussion Group Topics

- Reluctant test takers
- Students with disabilities (such as ADD)
- Pros and cons of high stakes tests
- Strategies parents already use at home to encourage academic achievement
- How to balance academics with extra-curricular activities
- How to read a report of your teen's standardized test score
- Impact of a job on academic achievement
- Gender-specific test preparation strategies

THE INS AND OUTS OF CHANGE

Parents are well equipped to serve as change agents, working to create public schools in which the dynamics of natural learning and the resources of the institution can combine to provide a supportive and challenging environment for all students. Hard work, patience, and resilience are required to initiate and sustain meaningful change. This section will cover the roles and relationships of three groups: core group, volunteers, and educators. Each of these groups must be involved in a thoughtful and timely way in the change process. Informed, involved parents also have an important role to play in the larger picture of school reform.

Informed and involved parents play an important role in school reform.

Core Group

The members of a core group often begin their work with a short-term goal in mind, but as they learn more, larger issues emerge and a long-term commitment to change takes shape. Initiatives for change in school policy and practice typically originate from a handful of people who have a strong vision of how school ought to be.

Let's say that you aren't sure what the consequences of doing well or poorly on your state's test are for your teenager. You discuss your concern with a few other parents whom you like and respect. They're not sure either. You've read the first four chapters of this book, so you're familiar with the language of standards and standardized testing, and you know you should start with the teacher. One teacher points out that the results are included on the student's transcript and that colleges will look at this. Another assures you that the test measures only districts and schools, not individuals. A third teacher complains about how much time is spent preparing students for the test at the expense of the regular curriculum. You are concerned by these inconsistencies, so you and your group make an appointment with the principal to learn more. When you sit down in the conference room with the principal, you are already acting as a core group. When you become a member of such a group, you will find yourself investing significant time and energy in order to achieve your goal. You will learn that real change happens slowly, because a desire for change has to reach a "critical mass" of people before it will actually occur.

Volunteers

The task of the core group is to provide as many people as possible with an opportunity to experience a desire for change. This process begins with volunteers—people who are somewhat concerned, but not enough so as to take the initiative to ask questions and gather information. The core group provides the information through workshops and discussion groups. In addition to disseminating information, these workshops and groups create a network. The volunteers will talk about what they have learned amongst one another and with people who did not attend, gradually increasing the number of people who are aware of the issue. Eventually this number will reach *critical mass.*

For teachers, critical mass is about two thirds of the total faculty, because teachers have to get close to consensus before enough pressure to change is brought to bear on those who want to retain the status quo. Among parents, critical mass is likely to be reached much sooner, because it takes relatively few parents speaking out about an issue to make other parents (and educators) pay attention. When critical mass is reached, the expectations that supported the status quo will shift, and change will already be underway.

Educators

You can have a significant positive impact by changing the way parents think about your issue. Your teenager will benefit from your increased knowledge and will take (secret) pleasure in your activism. These are important rewards for your time and effort. However, your ultimate goal is to change the beliefs of school administrators and the behaviors of teachers. Educators are rightly wary of a hue and cry that is really just the voice of one disgruntled parent magnified by sympathetic friends and neighbors. If your issue is perceived in this way, educators will band together to resist you.

At some point your vision will have to become large enough so that you are no longer primarily motivated by whether or not the change you desire occurs in time to impact your own teenager's experience in school. Because real changes occur in educational institutions so slowly, your child may very well graduate before change reaches the classroom. One reason that parents have not had quite the impact on school policy and practice you might expect is that your relationship with an individual school tends to endure only as long as you have students in it. Educators, knowing that parents come and go, may simply try to wait you out. You have to become something of a "super parent" concerned with the welfare of all teenagers, in order to achieve the credibility and patience needed to see an initiative for change through to implementation within the school.

Change is good, but it is difficult. Parents need to put themselves in the shoes of educators, and vice versa. As a parent who is in the know and in the loop, you can make the partnership between home and school a real and powerful force. Working together, we can make high school make sense to the young people whose days we share and for whom we wish the very best.

APPENDIXES: INFORMATION FOR PARENTS

A Glossary for Parents

Assessment: Measurement of student achievement at a specific point in time. It can be compared to a snapshot that captures a single moment in a student's academic career. Any type of task that a teacher uses to measure student knowledge or ability, from multiple-choice test to essay or project, qualifies as an assessment. You will want to find out from your child's teachers what kinds of assessments they use, how often they use them, how they align with the **content standards** (see below) for the course, and whether or not they help prepare the student for standardized state tests.

Authentic Assessment: Any assessment that involves students in "real world" activities. Assessments can be termed "authentic" if they approximate adult work activity (managing money, applying for a fictional job, etc.) or if they immerse students in real-life situations (composing letters to the newspaper editor on current issues, etc.). Since many of the new state tests use "authentic tasks," you may want to ask what the student's coursework is doing to help him or her prepare to do such tasks, and what you can do to support your teenager at home.

Benchmark: Standard by which something can be measured or judged. In education, benchmarks are samples of student work that set a standard by which other students' work can be judged. Referring to benchmarks gives both students and parents the opportunity to examine work which has met the standard; they show what an excellent product looks like. When you meet with your child's teachers, ask if the course has a set of benchmarks to examine, and how the teachers use them in instruction.

Content Standard: Statement of what students should know and be able to do at the end of a course. It indicates what students should learn and what kind of learning activities the teacher needs to provide. Content standards usually head the curriculum description; therefore, all the learning activities of the course should help students to meet those standards. You are entitled to see the curriculum for each course your child takes, and should feel free to ask questions about how the teacher accomplishes the content standards through daily class work.

Criterion-Referenced Test (CRT): A test that specifies a particular goal for students to achieve. A criterion-referenced test lists the characteristics of student work that demonstrate mastery. That list should be available to students and parents to help them understand what the task demands. When you discuss standardized tests with a teacher, you may need to ask which tests are criterion-referenced.

Evaluation: Analysis of student achievement over a period of time. The term is often used interchangeably with **assessment,** but it more specifically refers to long-term student work, such as a portfolio of art or writing, or a project that demands that the student use an entire semester's worth of learning to complete.

Exit Exam: A **high stakes test** given to students to measure whether they have mastered the necessary information to graduate high school. It is "high stakes" for students insofar as a diploma is the reward for passing the exam.

High Stakes Test: Any assessment with real consequences, in the form of rewards, sanctions, or intervention, attached to performance. Often, the outcome of a high stakes test determines whether or not the student will be promoted to the next grade or graduate (see **exit exam**). In some states, the "stakes" in question vary. Students who perform well, for example, may receive special recognition or monetary rewards; those performing poorly may be remanded to summer school. Schools and school districts are not immune to the consequences of high stakes tests either, as the results of such tests are often used to determine the amount of funding that school receives. You should inquire as to the consequences, if any, of your state's assessment.

Holistic Scoring: A technique that is more concerned with the whole than with analysis or separation into parts. Readers of essays and other written tests who score holistically assign a score based on their impression of the work as a whole. In contrast, traditional assessment of writing usually analyzes parts, such as outline, thesis, organization, spelling, etc. In standardized tests, holistic scoring is done by a minimum of two readers who receive training in the criteria for scoring. This is done to ensure consistency and fairness. It is important to ask which assessments are scored holistically.

Norm-Referenced Test (NRT): A test that compares an individual's score to the scores of a group of individuals. Test makers analyze the scores of a representative reference group who took the test beforehand, and determine percentiles of achievement. Therefore, students' achievements are being compared to the achievements of the students in that reference group. Norm-referenced assessments like the SAT and the ACT have raised controversy in the past when questions surfaced about how representative their reference groups are. NRTs such as the Stanford 9 and ITBS are also known as "off-the-shelf" tests.

Performance Assessment: Task that requires a student to demonstrate what he or she knows and is able to do. There is some similarity to an authentic assessment, but students may be asked to demonstrate knowledge strictly related to the academic content of a course without necessarily engaging in real-world activities. Teachers are often very proud of the performance assessments they have created, and are happy to display them when they meet with parents. You will want to look at them in the context of the content standards to see if they are in alignment.

Performance Standard: Statement that describes the individual tasks a student performs to demonstrate that he or she has met the **content standards**. Good performance standards give clear descriptions of what the teacher expects and show students how to meet those expectations. They should be published well in advance of the task so that students and parents can ask questions to clarify their understanding of what is expected.

Reliability: Consistency of test scores. A test that is reliable will produce consistent results. Students who take two different forms of the same test given in the same year should get similar scores on both forms. The test maker must provide documentation to the school that the test is reliable.

Rubric: A set of concise descriptors used for assessing student work, often organized in a grid to provide descriptors for four to six levels of achievement. Rubrics exist in many forms, but all give very specific descriptions of what student work should look like. Good rubrics help educators be more specific in assessing student work. They should be available to students in advance of doing a performance task so that they understand what is expected of them and how to meet those expectations. A good question to ask teachers is whether they use rubrics, and if so, how often, and whether they give them to students with enough advance notice to be helpful in completing the task.

Validity: Assurance that a test actually measures what it is supposed to measure. For example, if a test is supposed to measure students' knowledge of basic French grammar, it is invalid if it uses advanced vocabulary. Just as with **reliability**, test makers must document the validity of the test.

Web Resource Directory

Achieve, Inc.
www.achieve.org

Achieve is a private organization composed of members of the business community who hosted the most recent education summit. The Website includes extensive data banks that permit comparison of state standards. "Since 1998, Achieve has worked with 20 states to examine both the quality of their academic standards and the match between those standards and state assessments" (Edwards, 33).

AFT K–12 Teachers, Educational Issues Department
www.aft.org/edissues/standards99/

This site links to the American Federation of Teachers' 1999 Report "Making Standards Matter." The report not only discusses the national status of the standards movement but also reviews the standards produced by each state. While the perspective presented here does not necessarily reflect the views of other educational organizations, it does provide an interesting analysis. We also suggest you read the reply of your own state department of education to the AFT report (also housed at this URL location). Be sure to check the AFT site for its posting of the July 2001 report.

Association for Supervision and Curriculum Development
www.ascd.org

The organization's homepage has links to a variety of articles, resources, and commentaries on current practices in education.

Building Community Partnerships for Learning
eric-web.tc.columbia.edu/families/strong/

This section of the ERIC Website based on *Strong Families, Strong Schools* includes review of key research findings, examples of family involvement efforts that are working, and concrete ways in which different participants in the family involvement partnership can help achieve success.

Developing Educational Standards
PutnamValleySchools.org/Standards.html

This site is devoted to developing educational standards. It provides links to standards by state and by subject, to state departments of education, and to a variety of related sites.

Education Commission of the States
www.ecs.org

The Education Commission of the States (ECS) is a national, nonprofit organization that helps legislators, education officials, and others develop and implement policies to improve student learning at all levels. This Website includes issue sections designed to give you a comprehensive picture of the education topic that interests you, and includes news about what states are doing, the best publications available on the topic, and lists of other Websites with good information.

Education Week
www.edweek.org/context/states/

This will link you to an online version of *Education Week*'s state-by-state fact sheet, with comprehensive information on your state, including statistics, key players, legislative updates, *Ed Week* reports, and state news.

Eisenhower National Clearinghouse
www.enc.org

This site contains state frameworks and national guidelines for teaching and curriculum in math and science.

Learning Network Parent Channel
familyeducation.com

This site includes interactive information for parents, including polls, discussion groups, and articles on education.

The Nation's Report Card
www.nces.ed.gov/nationsreportcard/

This is the main Website for the National Assessment of Educational Progress (NAEP), an organization that has provided information and results on what students know and are able to do since 1969. By monitoring and communicating results of student performance, the NAEP continues to facilitate the progress of education.

Partnership for Family Involvement in Education
www.pfie.ed.gov

The Partnership works to create stronger connections between school, family, and community. This site enables you to research a particular school district as well as effective strategies you can use to get involved. From publications to calendars to networks, this site helps you learn how to get involved in your teenager's school and foster the quality of learning for all members of the school community.

Public Agenda Online
www.publicagenda.org

This site provides citizens with research tools to explore education policy in more detail.

High Stakes
High School Exam Map

All states except Iowa—where testing decisions are left to individual districts—have standardized assessments (if not exit exams) for high school students. At the time of this book's publication, there are nineteen states that place considerably high stakes on their tests: Students must pass or they will not be allowed to graduate from high school. With at least nine other states intending to follow suit, accountability is clearly emerging as a major theme in national education.

These states currently have legislation in place that requires high school students to pass the state standardized test in order to graduate:

Alabama	New Jersey
Florida	New Mexico
Georgia	New York
Indiana	North Carolina
Louisiana	Ohio
Maryland	South Carolina
Massachusetts	Tennessee
Minnesota	Texas
Mississippi	Virginia
Nevada	

The map on the next page illustrates the growing trend towards high stakes testing.

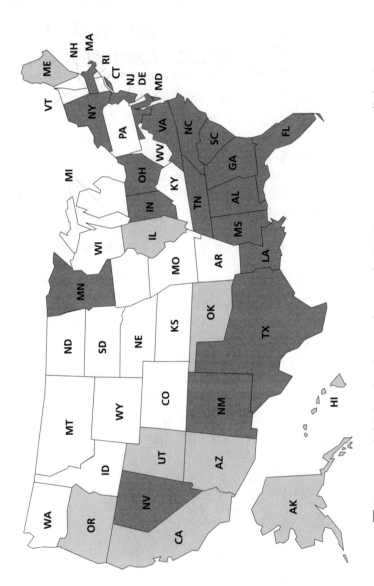

■ States with high school tests that students must pass to earn a diploma
▨ States with plans to implement high school exit exams

High School Tests
Administered by Your State

Many state assessments are referred to by acronym, or even by an altogether "other" name. The following chart can help clear any confusion and tell you which state tests your high schooler will be given, and in which grade. (Please note that all of the information is current as of this book's publication date.)

State	Test Name	Grade(s)
Alabama	Alabama High School Graduation Exam (AHSGE), Third Edition	10
	Stanford Achievement Test, Ninth Edition (Stanford 9)	9, 10, 11
Alaska	High School Graduation Qualifying Examination (HSGQE)	11
Arizona	Arizona's Instrument to Measure Standards (AIMS)	11
	Stanford Achievement Test, Ninth Edition (Stanford 9)	9, 10, 11
Arkansas	Arkansas Criterion-Referenced Test (ACRT)	11
	Stanford Achievement Test, Ninth Edition (Stanford 9)	10
California	Standardized Testing and Reporting (STAR) [also called Stanford 9]	9, 10, 11
	Golden State Exams (GSE)	HS
	California High School Exit Exam (CAHSEE)	10

State	Test Name	Grade(s)
Colorado	Colorado State Assessment Program (CSAP)	9, 10
	American College Testing (ACT)	11
Connecticut	Connecticut Academic Performance Test (CAPT)	11
Delaware	Delaware Student Testing Program (DSTP)	10
Florida	Florida Comprehensive Assessment Test (FCAT)	10
Georgia	Georgia High School Graduation Test (GHSGT)	11, 12
Hawaii	Stanford Achievement Test, Ninth Edition (Stanford 9)	9
Idaho	Iowa Test of Basic Skills (ITBS)	9, 10, 11
	Direct Writing Assessment (DWA)	11
Illinois	Prairie State Achievement Exam (PSAE)	11
Indiana	Indiana Statewide Testing for Educational Progress (ISTEP+)	11
Iowa	Iowa does not currently have a statewide high school testing program.	
Kansas	Kansas Assessment Program (KAP)	10, 11
Kentucky	Comprehensive Test of Basic Skills (CTBS/5 or TerraNova)	9
	Kentucky Core Content Test (KCCT)	10, 11
Louisiana	Graduate Exit Exam for the 21st Century (GEE 21)	10, 11
Maine	Maine Educational Assessment (MEA)	11
Maryland	Maryland Functional Tests (MFT)	9, 11
	Maryland High School Assessments [debuts 2002]	10, 11, 12
Massachusetts	Massachusetts Comprehensive Assessment System (MCAS)	10
Michigan	Michigan Educational Assessment Program (MEAP)	11

State	Test Name	Grade(s)
Minnesota	Basic Standards Tests (BST)	8, 10
Mississippi	Mississippi Subject Area Testing Program (MSATP) [debuts 2001; will eventually replace FLE]	HS
	Functional Literacy Examination (FLE)	11
Missouri	Missouri Assessment Program (MAP)	10, 11
Montana	Montana does not currently have a statewide high school testing program. Districts choose between 3 approved norm-referenced tests: Comprehensive Test of Basic Skills (CTBS 5/TerraNova); Iowa Test of Basic Skills (ITBS); Stanford 9	11
Nebraska	Nebraska does not currently have a statewide high school testing program.	
Nevada	High School Proficiency Exam (HSPE)	11, 12
New Hampshire	New Hampshire Educational Improvement Assessment Program (NHEIAP)	10
New Jersey	High School Proficiency Test (HSPT)	11
	High School Proficiency Assessment (HSPA) [debuts 2004–2005; will replace HSPT]	11
New Mexico	New Mexico High School Competency Examination (NMHSCE)	11
	CTBS 5/Terra Nova	9
New York	New York State Regents Exams	10, 11, 12
North Carolina	End-of Course Tests (EOC)	10, 11, 12
	North Carolina High School Exit Exam (NCHSEE) [debuts 2004; also called Essential Skills Exit Exam]	10
North Dakota	Comprehensive Test of Basic Skills (CTBS/5 or TerraNova)	10

State	Test Name	Grade(s)
Ohio	Ohio Proficiency Test (OPT)	9, 12
	High School Graduation Qualifying Examination (HSGQE) [Debuts 2002; will replace OPT]	10
Oklahoma	Oklahoma Core Curriculum Tests (OCCT)	11
Oregon	Oregon Statewide Assessments (OSA)	10
Pennsylvania	Pennsylvania System of School Assessment (PSSA)	11
Rhode Island	New Standards Reference Exam (NSRE)	9, 10
South Carolina	Palmetto Achievement Challenge Tests (PACT) [debuts 2001]	10
South Dakota	Stanford Writing Assessment (SWA)	9
	Stanford Achievement Test, Ninth Edition (Stanford 9)	11
Tennessee	Gateway Tests [debuts 2001]	9, 10, 11, 12
Texas	Texas Assessment of Academic Skills (TAAS)	10 [11 in 2003]
	End of Course Tests (EOC)	10, 11, 12
Utah	Stanford Achievement Test, Ninth Edition (Stanford 9)	11
Vermont	Vermont's Comprehensive Assessment System (VCAS)	10, 11
Virginia	Standards of Learning (SOL) [also known as End of Course (EOC) exams]	10, 11, 12
	Stanford Achievement Test, Ninth Edition (Stanford 9)	11
Washington	Washington Assessment of Student Learning (WASL)	10
West Virginia	Stanford Achievement Test, Ninth Edition (Stanford 9)	9, 10, 11
Wisconsin	Wisconsin Knowledge and Concepts Examination (WKCE)	10
	High School Graduation Test (HSGT) [debuts 2002]	10
Wyoming	Wyoming Comprehensive Assessment System (WyCAS)	11

State by State Survey

	Type of Test				Alignment with Standards			
STATE	**MC**	**SA**	**ER/Eng**	**ER/O**	**English**	**Math**	**History**	**Science**
Alabama	×				×	×	×	×
Alaska	×	×	×		×	×		
Arizona	×		×		×	×		
Arkansas	×	×	×		×	×		
California	×				×	×	×	×
Colorado	×	×	×		×	×		
Connecticut	×	×	×	×	×	×	×	×
Delaware	×	×	×		×	×	×	×
Florida	×	×	×		×	×		
Georgia	×		×		×	×	×	×
Hawaii	×	×	×		×	×		
Idaho	×		×		×			
Illinois	×		×		×	×	×	×

Type of Standardized Test Used in High Schools and the Alignment of Each Test with Standards

MC = multiple-choice
SA = short answer
ER/Eng = extended response in English portion of test
ER/O = extended response in other portions of the test

STATE	Type of Test				Alignment with Standards			
	MC	SA	ER/Eng	ER/O	English	Math	History	Science
Indiana	X	X	X		X	X		
Iowa	X							
Kansas	X				X	X	X	X
Kentucky	X	X	X	X	X	X	X	X
Louisiana	X	X	X		X	X		
Maine	X	X	X	X	X	X	X	X
Maryland	X	X	X		X	X	X	X
Massachusetts	X	X	X		X	X	X	X
Michigan	X	X	X	X	X	X	X	X
Minnesota		X						
Mississippi	X	X	X		X	X	X	X
Missouri	X	X	X		X	X	X	X
Montana	X							
Nebraska		X			X			
Nevada	X		X		X	X		
New Hampshire	X	X	X		X	X	X	X
New Jersey	X	X	X					
New Mexico	X	X	X		X	X	X	X
New York	X	X	X	X	X	X	X	X
North Carolina	X		X		X	X	X	X
North Dakota	X				X	X		
Ohio	X		X		X	X	X	X
Oklahoma	X				X		X	
Oregon	X	X	X		X	X		X
Pennsylvania	X	X	X		X	X		

MC = multiple-choice
SA = short answer
ER/Eng = extended response in English portion of test
ER/O = extended response in other portions of the test

STATE	Type of Test				Alignment with Standards			
	MC	SA	ER/Eng	ER/O	English	Math	History	Science
Rhode Island	X	X	X		X	X		
South Carolina	X		X					
South Dakota	X		X					
Tennessee	X		X		X	X		
Texas	X	X	X		X	X	X	X
Utah	X	X	X		X	X		X
Vermont	X	X	X		X	X		
Virginia	X		X		X	X	X	X
Washington	X	X	X		X	X		X
West Virginia	X		X					
Wisconsin	X	X	X					
Wyoming	X	X	X		X	X		

MC = multiple-choice
SA = short answer
ER/Eng = extended response in English portion of test
ER/O = extended response in other portions of the test

The information in this chart is based on *Education Week*'s "Quality Counts 2001." Reprinted with permission from *Education Week*. Vol. 20, No. 17, January 11, 2001.

A Brief History of High School

1821 The first public high school opens in Boston (boys only).

1825 Illinois enacts the first public school tax.

1827 Massachusetts requires towns with more than 500 families to establish high schools, and towns begin to provide separate high schools for girls.

1850 The Industrial Revolution inspires schools to adopt the factory model for education.

1911 Alfred Binet develops a series of tests designed to measure intelligence.

1918 School attendance becomes compulsory in all states.

1920 High schools use intelligence tests to place students in learning "tracks."

1947 The Educational Testing Service is established to provide standardized tests for college admissions.

1950 American high schools consolidate to offer a wider range of programs.

1954 Brown v. Board of Education outlaws segregation in public schools.

1957 Sputnik inspires a more rigorous curriculum-based education in math and science.

1965 The Elementary and Secondary School Act (ESEA) is passed and becomes the single largest source of federal assistance to disadvantaged students, schools, and communities.

1983 *A Nation at Risk* is published and recommends, among other things, higher academic standards for all students.

1989 U.S. governors establish education goals in six areas.

1992 President Clinton adds two goals, challenges the nation's educators and parents to achieve all eight by the year 2000, and calls the program "Goals 2000."

1994   The ESEA is reauthorized and includes the $8.6 billion-a-year Title I program, which requires states to set up systems of standards and aligned assignments and to demonstrate yearly progress.

2001   Newly elected president George W. Bush makes education reform his first priority with the release of his "No Child Left Behind" plan.

National Education Goals— "Goals 2000"

Goals 2000

Goal 1—Ready to Learn
All children in America will start school ready to learn.

Goal 2—School Completion
The high school graduation rate will increase to at least 90 percent.

Goal 3—Student Achievement and Citizenship
All students will leave grades 4, 8, and 12 having demonstrated competency over challenging subject matter including English, mathematics, science, foreign languages, civics and government, economics, the arts, history, and geography.

Goal 4—Teacher Education and Professional Development
The nation's teaching force will have access to programs for the continued improvement of their professional skills and the opportunity to acquire the knowledge and skills needed to instruct and prepare all American students for the next century.

Goal 5—Mathematics and Science
U.S. students will be first in the world in mathematics and science achievement.

Goal 6—Adult Literacy and Lifelong Learning
Every adult will be literate and will possess the knowledge to compete in a global economy and exercise the responsibilities of citizenship.

Goal 7—Safe, Disciplined, and Alcohol- and Drug-Free Schools
Every U.S. school will be free of drugs, violence, and the unauthorized presence of firearms and alcohol.

Goal 8—Parental Participation
Every school will promote partnerships that will increase parental involvement and participation in promoting the growth of children.

Works Cited

Achieve, Inc. Online at www.achieve.org.

American Federation of Teachers, Educational Issues Department. *Making Standards Matter*, 1999. Online at www.aft.org/edissues/standards99/.

Bicouvaris, Mary V. "National Standards for History: The Struggles Behind the Scenes." *Clearing House*, January/February 1996, 136–139.

Boser, Ulrich. "Teaching to the Test?" *Education Week*, 7 June 2000, 1–10.

Dykstra, Joan and Arnold F. Fege. "Not Without Parents." *Education Week on the Web*, 19 March 1997, online at www.edweek.org/ew/1997/25dykstr.h16.

Edwards, Virginia B., ed. "Quality Counts 2001: A Better Balance." *Education Week*, 11 January 2001, 8, 33.

ERIC Clearinghouse on Urban Education, Urban Education Web. *Strong Families, Strong Schools*, 1999. Online at eric-web.tc.columbia.edu/families/strong/.

Feldman, Sandra. "The Uproar Over Testing." *American Teacher*, September 2000, 5.

Gatto, John Taylor. "We Need Less School, Not More." *Whole Earth Review*, Winter 1993, 54–63.

Goldstein, Andrew. "Paging All Parents." *Time*, 3 July 2000, online at www.time.com/time/magazine/article/0,9171,48095,00.html

Henriques, Diana B. and Jacques Steinberg. "Right Answer; Wrong Score: Test Flaws Take Toll." *New York Times*, 20 May 2001, 1, 34–35.

Hoff, David. "As Expectations Rise, Definition of Cheating Blurs." *Education Week*, 21 June 2000, 1, 14–15.

Holland, Holly. "Commentary: Putting Parents in Their Place." *Education Week*, 22 September 1999, 33, 44.

Kohn, Alfie. "Confusing Harder with Better: Why the 'Tougher Standards' Movement Is Undermining Our Schools." *Education Week*, 15 September 1999, 52, 68.

National Assessment of Educational Progress K–12 Practitioners' Circle, Parents. Online at www.nces.ed.gov/practitioners/parents.asp.

Olson, Lynn. "States Ponder New Forms of Diploma." *Education Week*, 21 June 2000, 1, 30.

Public Agenda. "Playing Their Parts: What Parents and Teachers Really Mean by Parental Involvement," 1999. Online at www.publicagenda.org/specials/parent/parent.htm.

Rhodes, Steve. "Getting Testy." *Chicago*, February 2000, 41–43.

Schmoker, Michael. *Results: The Key to Continuous School Improvement*. Alexandria: Association for Supervision and Curriculum Development, 1996.

Shea, Christopher. "It's Come to This." *Teacher Magazine*, May/June 2000, 34.

Texas Education Agency. *Interpreting Assessment Reports*, 2000. Texas Student Assessment Program. Online at www.tea.state.tx.us.

Tomlinson, Carol Ann. *The Differentiated Classroom, Responding to the Needs of All Learners*. Alexandria, VA: The Association for Supervision and Curriculum Development, 1999: 18.

U.S. Department of Education. *A Nation at Risk*, 1983. Online at ed.gov/pubs/NatAtRisk/risk.html.

Vander Ark, Tom and Tony Wagner. "Between Hope and Despair." *Education Week*, 21 June 2000, 50, 76.

Zernike, Kate. "In Suburbs, It's Location, Location . . . Test Scores." *New York Times*, 3 June 2000, B1–B2.

Notes

How Did We Do? Grade Us.

Thank you for choosing a Kaplan book. Your comments and suggestions are very useful to us. Please answer the following questions to assist us in our continued development of high-quality resources to meet your needs.

The title of the Kaplan book I read was: _____

My name is: _____

My address is: _____

_____

My e-mail address is: _____

What overall grade would you give this book?   (A) (B) (C) (D) (F)

How relevant was the information to your goals?   (A) (B) (C) (D) (F)

How comprehensive was the information in this book?   (A) (B) (C) (D) (F)

How accurate was the information in this book?   (A) (B) (C) (D) (F)

How easy was the book to use?   (A) (B) (C) (D) (F)

How appealing was the book's design?   (A) (B) (C) (D) (F)

What were the book's strong points? _____

How could this book be improved? _____

Is there anything that we left out that you wanted to know more about?

Would you recommend this book to others?   ☐ YES   ☐ NO

Other comments: _____

_____

_____

Do we have permission to quote you?   ☐ YES   ☐ NO

Thank you for your help.
Please tear out this page and mail it to:

Managing Editor
Kaplan, Inc.
888 Seventh Avenue
New York, NY 10106

KAPLAN

Thanks!

About
KAPLAN
Educational Centers

Kaplan Educational Centers is one of the nation's leading providers of premier education and career services. Kaplan is a wholly owned subsidiary of The Washington Post Company.

TEST PREPARATION & ADMISSIONS

Kaplan's nationally recognized test prep courses cover more than 20 standardized tests, including secondary school, college and graduate school entrance exams and foreign language and professional licensing exams. In addition, Kaplan offers private tutoring and comprehensive, one-to-one admissions and application advice for students applying to graduate programs. Kaplan also provides information and guidance on the financial aid process.

SCORE! EDUCATIONAL CENTERS

SCORE! after-school learning centers help K-8 students build confidence, academic and goal-setting skills in a motivating, sports-oriented environment. Its cutting-edge, interactive curriculum continually assesses and adapts to each child's academic needs and learning style. Enthusiastic Academic Coaches serve as positive role models, creating a high-energy atmosphere where learning is exciting and fun. SCORE! Prep provides in-home, one-on-one tutoring for high school academic subjects and standardized tests.

KAPLAN LEARNING SERVICES

Kaplan Learning Services provides customized assessment, education and professional development programs to K-12 schools and universities.

KAPLAN INTERNATIONAL PROGRAMS

Kaplan services international students and professionals in the U.S. through a series of intensive English language and test preparation programs. These programs are offered at Kaplan City Centers and four new campus-based centers in California, Washington and New York via Kaplan/LCP International Institute. Kaplan and Kaplan/LCP offer specialized services to sponsors including placement at top American universities, fellowship management, academic monitoring and reporting, and financial administration.

KAPLAN PUBLISHING

Kaplan Publishing produces books, software and online services. Kaplan Books, a joint imprint with Simon & Schuster, publishes titles in test preparation, admissions, education, career development and life skills; Kaplan and Newsweek jointly publish guides on getting into college, finding the right career, and helping your child succeed in school. Through an alliance with Knowledge Adventure, Kaplan publishes educational software for the K-12 retail and school markets.

KAPLAN PROFESSIONAL

Kaplan Professional provides recruitment and training services for corporate clients and individuals seeking to advance their careers. Member units include Kaplan Professional Career Services, the largest career fair provider in North America; Perfect Access/CRN, which delivers software education and consultation for law firms and businesses; HireSystems, which provides web-based hiring solutions; and Kaplan Professional Call Center Services, a total provider of services for the call center industry.

DISTANCE LEARNING DIVISION

Kaplan's distance learning programs include Concord School of Law, the nation's first online law school; and National Institute of Paralegal Arts and Sciences, a leading provider of degrees and certificates in paralegal studies and legal nurse consulting.

COMMUNITY OUTREACH

Kaplan provides educational resources to thousands of financially disadvantaged students annually, working closely with educational institutions, not-for-profit groups, government agencies and other grass roots organizations on a variety of national and local support programs. Kaplan enriches local communities by employing high school, college and graduate students, creating valuable work experiences for vast numbers of young people each year.

Want more information about our services, products or the nearest Kaplan center?

1 **Call our nationwide toll-free numbers:**

1-800-KAP-TEST for information on our test prep courses, private tutoring and admissions consulting

1-800-KAP-ITEM for information on our books and software

1-888-KAP-LOAN* for information on student loans

2 **Connect with us online:**

On the web, go to:
www.kaptest.com
Via email:
info@kaplan.com

3 **Write to:**

Kaplan
888 Seventh Avenue
New York, NY 10106

KAPLAN